"One cannot and must not try to erase the past merely because it does not fit the present."

Golda Meir

଼

SOROS

VS.

TRUMP

The Men & The Issues
Dividing America

Hadassah Jacobs

Soros vs.Trump

Published in the United States, 2022 by Hadassah Jacobs

Print ISBN: 9798360411406
First Edition, 2022

For articles, interviews, permissions & speaking engagements, please email:

hadas@hadassahjacobs.com

Or subscribe to my email list www.hadassahjacobs.com

to receive the latest commentary on current events.

CONTENTS

NOTE TO READERS

This publication contains the opinions and ideas of its author. I have done my best to support all research, comments, and criticisms with quotes from articles, journals, books, and websites. The book attempts to answer the plethora of questions surrounding the 2016 election and its aftermath. The author's intention is to help the American citizen and all who watched the 2016 and 2020 elections in utter disbelief to understand "what was going on," "what is going on," and "what just happened?" In other words, why Trump?

The issues discussed in this book are controversial and often connected to influential individuals that either hold prestigious positions in Washington or have the ear of those who do. It is not the author's intent to disparage these individuals but to present the facts surrounding their connections with the men and the issues dividing America. This is not an "anti-anyone or anti-any party" book. The author harbors no animosity or hatred towards the mentioned persons or organizations.

It is not the intent of the author to incite hatred or any other attitude that would prove to be disrespectful or anti-American. The insights and expressions made throughout these pages are not necessarily the views of the contributing authors, individuals, or organizations mentioned or cited within this book. The content is original to the author.

This book is dedicated to my mother. She wrote the script for life and love in my heart through her continual example of courage, strength, and sheer determination. From a young age, my mother taught me social responsibility. From PTA to Politics, my mother was involved.

One of my favorite memories was the yearly *Toys for Tots* drive. Every holiday season, we went through all our toys, made piles, and bagged them according to a category, i.e., stuffed animals, puzzles, and games. We then went shopping to buy new games for the needy children we were personally sponsoring.

On the big day, we schlepped all our treasures to the Community Center and met the children we sponsored. In just a couple of hours, all our plans and preparations were over. But the lessons learned by helping others less fortunate through caring, sharing, and sacrifice are eternal.

This is the America I grew up in. Time and time again, I watched my mother sacrifice the little she had for those who needed it more. My mom taught me what it truly meant to be an American.

A PERSONAL NOTE . . .

ꝏ

Why Soros vs. Trump? This is the question I attempt to answer throughout the book. Many say "knowledge is power;" however, I have come to believe that "understanding is power." And for this reason, Soros vs. Trump exists.

This book started with a question I received on Facebook from a dear friend:

Hi Hadas, I just wanted to get your take on Donald Trump; it looks like he will be the Republican nominee. Is this a good thing, and if so, why? A lot of people here are torn, they don't like Hillary or the Democrats, but they were hoping for someone better than Donald to be the change we were hoping for after eight years of Obama.

I always value your opinion and knowledge.

Thank You, Larry

I wrote a quick response as to why I knew Trump would be the Republican nominee and ended with this statement:

> As for other issues, such as character, repentance remarks, policy, women, immigration, Israel, trade, and everything else the media, GOP, and Conservatives challenge him on, I will discuss in a separate letter.

This book is the "separate letter."

What started as a letter to clarify the character and position statements of President-elect Donald Trump turned into a book about the men, organizations, and ideologies working in the shadows to undermine the foundations of America.

Every time I dug a little deeper into the challenging presidential race between Trump and Clinton, one man's name appeared, George Soros.

Soros was a significant donor behind the Obama, Clinton, and Biden elections, yet so little is known about him or his global network. I was first introduced to him through the Glen Beck Show on FOX. I still remember my boss ridiculing Beck's insane summation of Soros. But I didn't think it was insane; he was spot on. Soros fascinated me then, and he still does today.

Every twist and turn surrounding the Trump campaigns led me to Soros. And, at some point, I finally understood what was at stake and whom Trump was really campaigning against. In 2016 and 2020, Soros was the real candidate running against Trump.

Within the pages of this book, you will be introduced to both George Soros and Donald Trump in the most objective way possible. You will also have a front-row seat to the eight years of Obama's presidency. A presidency that sowed the seeds of radical change being witnessed in Washington today.

Understanding these developments and their ideological underpinnings is more crucial today than at any other time in U.S. history. They cannot be ignored by Americans or elected officials if America is to survive as a leading democracy.

What you are about to read concerns the deep and secret things—that which is obscure to the human eye. These hidden things belong to Hashem, but once revealed, they belong to us. What we do with what's revealed is up to us.

In closing, allow me to share the scripted words M (Dame Judi Dench) used to defend the British Secret Service in her last James Bond movie, *Skyfall*. These words succinctly describe what I came to understand while writing *this book.*

I suppose that I see a different world than you do, and the truth is that what I see frightens me. I am frightened because our enemies are no longer known to us. They do

not exist on a map; they're not nations; they are individuals. Look around you; whom do you fear? Can you see a face, a uniform, a flag? No. Our world is not more transparent now; it's more opaque. It's in the shadows. That's where we must do battle.

I have one more thing to say. Here, today, I remember this, which I think is from Tennyson, "we are not now that strength which in the old days moved earth and heaven. That which we are, we are. One equal temper of heroic hearts made weak by time and fate, but strong in will to strive, to seek, to find and not to yield."

FOREWORD
by Bill Mehlman

ॐ

Hadassah Jacobs has given us in these pages an MRI of a U.S. Constitution on the cusp of free fall. Its precarious condition recalls Benjamin Franklin's prophetic reply to the question "What have we created here?" posed to him by a concerned observer at the close of the Constitutional Convention in Philadelphia in 1787. "A republic," Franklin replied, "if we can keep it."

For the better part of two-plus centuries, in war and peace, in good times and bad, we have managed to keep it, this constitutional anchor to which our rights and responsibilities are indispensably linked. Even in our worst moments, it has stood as an impenetrable shield against any threat to the collegial but equal and independent executive, legislative and judicial powers that have charted America's course. Mistakes along the way were inevitable, but the organic structure of the document produced in Philadelphia by the most remarkable group of men ever to create a nation always kept the gate open to course correction.

We have witnessed, over nearly two decades and most pointedly in the last eight years, an erosion of the concept of divided decision-making powers unprecedented in American history, compounded by the politicization of virtually every aspect of the nation's social and civil marketplace. They are in evidence wherever one looks, most prominently in the widespread displacement of the federal legislative process by executive decree; in an open-borders immigration stance that has made a mockery of national sovereignty; in the admission to our shores of hundreds of thousands of poorly vetted and virtually un-vetted immigrants from countries culturally prone to violence, and in the suspicion of whole government agencies being manipulated for political advantage.

On the social-civil side of the ledger, we have witnessed what can only be called an unholy alliance between the mainstream Protestant religious establishment and a political party wedded to abortion on demand, delusionary gender concepts, race obsession, income redistribution, confiscatory, job-killing taxation and a continued American retreat from its role as guardian of international peace and stability.

The cure for these ills is in the hands of the American people. As they sow, so shall they reap. But if it is the most lucid, measured portrayal of the challenges to a Constitutional democracy they seek, they will find it in this brilliant exposition by historian Hadassah Jacobs.

CHAPTER ONE

Spider webs, Cockatrice Eggs, and Vipers

"None calls for justice, nor any pleads for truth: they trust in vanity and speak lies; they conceive mischief and bring forth iniquity. They hatch cockatrice' eggs and weave the spider's web: he that eats of their eggs dies, and that which is crushed breaks out into a viper." Isaiah 59:4-5

℘

Whether it's the latest James Bond movie *Spectre* or a *House of Cards* episode, there is one thing for sure; you are watching webs of unfathomable evil being spun and unraveled. Let's face it, today's bad guys aren't the bad guys of the 1960s, '70s, or '80s. Today, they are narcissistic liars and master manipulators of everything evil. They make the villains in Dudley Do-Right look like saints.

If you have ever watched the *House of Cards*, even one episode, you understand that deep gnawing feeling in the pit of your stomach that screams—I am watching some bad stuff—real evil. And as the plot thickens, you might ask yourself, "does this really happen in Washington? Can one or two individuals wield that much power? And if so, how?"

Now, let's turn our attention to the movie *Spectre*, which boasts the following synopsis:

> A cryptic message from Bond's past sends him on a trail to Mexico City and Rome, where he infiltrates a secret meeting and uncovers the existence of the sinister organization Spectre. While M battles political forces to keep the Secret Service alive, Bond peels back the layers of deceit to untangle the web and reveal the chilling truth behind Spectre.

From Mexico to Rome, the web was spun. The more visible it became, the more Bond realized that it was all-encompassing—entangling everyone Spectre touched. Only truth could destroy the web, but to reach the truth, there had to be a reckoning with the past and a disdain for the present.

Think about it. Two fictional stories with plots utilizing the imagery of the spider web-spinning and capturing its victims in obscurity, unseen and, most importantly, invisible to the public eye. How the web is spun is masterfully portrayed in the *House of Cards,* and how the web is unraveled is painstakingly revealed in the movie *Spectre.*

That's fiction—thrilling, edge-of-your-seat fiction.

However, what the American people and the world witnessed throughout the 2016 and 2020 election campaigns is not fiction. From Mexico to Rome, the White House to the Kremlin—it's real. And you've had a spectacular front and center seat to Washington's web of evil.

So how did we get here? What is going on behind the scenes in Washington? Who are the men and organizations driving the radical shift in American politics? And how could a businessman like Donald Trump rise to become President of the United States?

ℍ

Cockatrice Eggs

For years, I've pondered the following verse from Isaiah 59:5, *"they hatch cockatrice' eggs, and weave the spider's web: he that eats of their eggs dies, and that which is crushed breaks out into a viper."*

Yet, it was not until Donald Trump challenged the status quo in Washington and its global political elites that I understood what the prophet Isaiah was trying to tell us.

The context surrounding this passage summarizes Israel's political and spiritual condition before the Babylonian exile. The nation had reached a state of lawlessness that left no other option but Divine intervention, a course correction directed by God, Himself. A pattern duly noted throughout Israel's history.

Isaiah 59 begins with the prophet telling the people that "the LORD's hand is still outstretched and His ear can still hear." In other words, God had not moved, and all His senses were working perfectly. He was still in their midst. Who had moved away from God, though, was Israel. Her sins and iniquities seriously impeded her relationship with the Almighty. As a nation, her hands were defiled with the blood of heinous crimes. Her lips knew nothing but lies, and her tongue spoke perversely.

At the root of Israel's unruliness was the absence of two essential pillars of society: *justice and truth*. And without those two pillars supporting the nation's collective conscience, the political elites were having a field day. Their transgressions were endless, from the shedding of innocent blood to destroying the Torah's (law) moral foundation. They pretended to want peace, but instead, they incited violence. Isaiah summed up their actions with these words "there is no judgment in their endeavors, and all their paths are crooked."[1]

Why was there no judgment? Because there was no truth, as God said, "And judgment is turned away backward, and justice stands afar off: for truth is fallen in the street, and equity cannot enter. Yes, truth fails; and he that departs from evil becomes a prey: the LORD saw it, and it displeased him that there was no judgment."[2]

When a nation loses its judgment—it can no longer find its way. It cannot discern right and wrong, good and evil, holy and perverse. It may have an abundance of help, from maps to navigational apps and motivational speakers to psychologists, but its people are lost in everyday life.

Judgment is not the same as "judging." You've heard of the phrase "sound judgment?" Well, it means "the ability to make sound decisions amidst conflicting circumstances."

You may remember the story of King Solomon, who had to judge two mothers and one baby. In brief, the story goes like this: Two mothers bore children at the same time. One night, one of the mothers smothered her baby while sleeping. So, she slipped into the room of the other mother and exchanged her dead child for the living one. In the morning, when they awoke, the mother of the living child knew that the dead child was not her baby, but the other mother insisted it was. Hence, the matter was brought to the king. He listened to their stories and said, "Divide the living child in two, and give half to the one and half to the other."

Immediately, the real birth mother cried, "give the living child to the other woman." The other mother responded, "no, divide it, let it not be mine or hers." Then Solomon commanded that the "living child be given to its true birth mother." How wise was that judgment? Solomon went straight to the source of truth, the heart.

Is it not written that "out of the abundance of the heart the mouth speaks?" This is an example of wise judgment—rightly dividing between the truth and the lie and providing a solution for the problem.

What struck me, and apparently, millions of other Americans when Donald Trump first stepped into the political arena was his ability to look through the smokescreen of the Washington elites and bring solution-based ideas to America's challenges. Yes, his rhetoric was crass, and yes, his speech was simple (for some, too simple), but his tongue was sharp like a sword exposing what was in the shadows.

The aftermath of Trump's first Republican Party presidential debates caused me to have an "aha moment" over Isaiah's spider webs and cockatrice eggs. My years of pondering Isaiah 59 were over. What happened? Trump stepped on a cockatrice egg. Have you ever heard of a cockatrice egg? Isaiah said that political elites who reject justice and judgment hatch them. What are they? They, my friends, are the eggs of poisonous serpents like the death adder or the viper that thrust out their tongues to kill their victims. The word "cockatrice" comes from the Hebrew root word, "צֶפַע (tseh'fah)," and it means "to extrude."

Did you know that the death adder has the most highly developed venom injecting mechanism of all snakes? Interestingly, they are not aggressive animals. They only inject venom when threatened, caught, or stepped on.[3] Furthermore, the death adder doesn't hunt its prey but lies in ambush and draws its prey to it. A death adder can strike, envenom its prey, and recoil in less than 0.15 seconds—that's less than 1/4 of a second.[4]

Did you happen to notice what happened within hours and days after Trump exposed the corruption of the Mexican government during his June 16th campaign announcement? Macy's dropped his clothing line, NBC and Univision (Spanish broadcaster) dropped the Ms. Universe and Ms. USA pageants,[5] and Serta dropped his mattress line. Then ESPN and NASCAR had their moment: ESPN pulled out of a golf outing at Trump National Golf Club in Los Angeles, and NASCAR reneged on a banquet scheduled at the Trump National Miami Doral resort.

Yes, Donald Trump stepped on one or two Washington cockatrice eggs, and out came the vipers.

Macy's, pressured by the organization MoveOn.org, told MSNBC, "In light of statements made by Donald Trump, which is inconsistent with Macy's values, we have decided to discontinue our business relationship with Mr. Trump . . .." Serta's rationale was, "Serta values diversity and does not agree with nor endorse the recent statements made by Mr. Trump." NBC said, "At NBC, respect and dignity for all people are the cornerstones of our values. Due to the recent derogatory statements by Donald Trump regarding immigrants, NBC Universal is ending its business relationship with Mr. Trump."[6]

As for ESPN and NASCAR, they just flowed with the politically correct wave of social justice.

About all of them, Trump wrote:

I have lost a lot during this Presidential run defending the people of the United States. I have always heard that it is very hard for a successful person to run for President. Macy's, NBC, Serta, and NASCAR have all taken the weak and very sad position of being politically correct even though they are wrong in terms of what is good for our country.[7]

Notably, these companies are all American-born, so their acts of disavowing Donald Trump over his immigration comments in a country of free speech, lead us to ask, "what was taking place behind the scenes?"

Let's start with Macy's.

MoveOn.org created a petition to intimidate Macy's into disenfranchising Trump. The petition read:

Macy's: Donald Trump does not reflect "the magic of Macy's." We urge you to sever ties with him. Macy's says it has a strong obligation to be "socially responsible" and that "actions speak louder than words." Indeed, it's time to act.[8]

Comparing Macy's lack of response to that of NBC's quick response, the petition released its adder's venom into its unsuspecting signees. It was a vilification of Trump to the first degree! Hatred was framed in such a way to make both Trump and Macy's look like full-fledged enemies of social responsibility.

Before we move beyond Macy's and into the heart of the events, let's ask, "could there be anything deceptively menacing about MoveOn.org?"

Well, as a matter of fact, yes. "The group acts as a front for wealthy Democrats. It was founded with the help of financier

George Soros who donated $1.46 million to get the organization rolling. Linda Pritzker of the Hyatt hotel family also gave the group a $4 million donation."[9]

Additionally, MoveOn.org has a problem with telling the truth. FactCheck.org duly noted that the organization had misled the public numerous times, particularly during election campaigns.

Do you remember MoveOn.org's Fat Cat TV AD that played during the Obama—Romney race?

It flaunted a few cute and cuddly fat cats while sending this subliminal message: "when the wealthiest 1% pay a fair tax rate like the rest of us, it keeps the American dream alive for everyone." Sounds just, doesn't it? Yes, but was it? MoveOn.org wanted you to believe those fat cats were millionaires and billionaires who were not paying their fair share. Yet, based on MoveOn.org's statistics, those fat cats were neither billionaires nor millionaires; they were the 1 million American households earning around $500,000. According to FactCheck, "this 1% was paying 10-20% more in income taxes than the rest of us."

Wouldn't you agree that MoveOn.org's use of cute and cuddly fat cats to deceive and manipulate the American people were dishonest?[10]

Another organization that has issues with MoveOn.org is PolitiFact.com PolitiFact.com has their famous Truth-O-Meter showing that only 36% of MoveOn's statements are accurate. The other 64% register half-truths or false, falling close to the red buzzer that sets off the siren shouting, "liar, liar, your pants are on fire."[11] All of that's bad, but bad becomes sinister when funding comes from Trump's arch enemy and America's number one subversionist,[12] George Soros.

MoveOn.org is one of Washington's cockatrice eggs.

Most people I speak with are unfamiliar with George Soros, so let's spend the remainder of this chapter looking at a key figure behind the Washington web and more than a few cockatrice eggs.

&

Meet George Soros

If you are a Glenn Beck fan or a politico, then you've probably heard of George Soros; otherwise, doubtful. You need to know who he is because he is in the shadows of the radical upheaval of a Constitutional America. Soros, a brilliant man, is not a patriotic American.

Even though you may not know him personally, you have encountered his mass political manipulation. Under the Obama administration, Soros left his imprint all over the country. Your first encounter was during the 2016 election campaign. Whenever there was a ridiculous outburst of protest in our nation Soros and his Open Society Foundation funded the organizations fueling the—Occupy Wall Street, Black Lives Matter, or Dump Trump. Even months into Trump's presidency, his agenda to derail and unseat Trump lingered with media bias, ANTIFA gatherings, and the Russian collusion dossier.[13]

So, who is Soros?

If you google him, your first read will be "George Soros, a Hungarian-American business magnate, investor, political activist, and author of Jewish-Hungarian ancestry and holds dual citizenship. He is chairman of Soros Fund Management." Another bio reads, "George Soros was born in Budapest, Hungary, on August 12, 1930. After surviving the Nazi invasion and occupation of Hungary in the early 1940s, Soros fled then-Communist-dominated Hungary in 1947 and made his way to England."

Both bio's make George Soros out to be a Hungarian Jew that survived the Holocaust and afterward forged a new life in England—very misleading, very misleading indeed. Yes, George Soros is a Hungarian Jew and a Holocaust survivor, but how he survived the Holocaust is another story. At thirteen, George posed as the godson of an official of Hungary's fascist government. As the godson, he was not exempt from turning Jews over to SS.[14][15] He was also involved in accompanying and, at times aiding his Nazi godfather in confiscating Jewish wealth. Concerning this phase of his life, Soros declared, "this was when my character was made."[16] This is a very telling statement.

When Soros was 14, his wealthy father "bribed a government official to take 14-year-old George in and swear that he was his Christian godson."[17] That's understandable, as a good father would do anything to ensure his family's safety.

So, who was the Nazi that his father bribed? Bambach, a Hungarian official who directly or indirectly reported to Francois Genoud, the Reich's Treasurer. During the war, Bambach took George with him to confiscate Jewish property, which allegedly connected him to Genoud. How or when George became connected to Genoud is unclear. What is known is that they became lifelong friends.

Francois Genoud met and funded Amin al-Husseini, the Grand Mufti of Jerusalem, under Hitler's orders during the war. Post-war, he managed the hidden Nazi treasury and financed the defense of many Nazis'[18] He also admitted to being the conspirator of the Palestinian hijacking of the Belgian Sabena Airlines Flight 571, as it flew from Vienna to Tel Aviv on May 8, 1972. He became the founder of the Arab Commercial Bank of Switzerland used to fund terrorism operations. Pamela Geller, a controversial figure herself, noted that "he may have even started his bank with the Nazi treasure that was stolen goods and gold from the Jews."[19] And if that's not enough to make your jaw drop, Genoud is on printed record saying that "Hitler wanted the movement to move from Nazism to Islamism and to carry on the National Socialism movement to gain control of the world and to exterminate Jews."[20] This is one of the men who influenced George Soros and helped shape his character. And notably, Soros likes to deal with people who oversee treasuries; first, Francois Genoud and secondly, former U.S. Secretary of the Treasury Jack Lew—coincidence?

In May of 2015, days after Soros warned Washington to succumb to China on the IMF currency basket, he was hacked by CyberBerkut.[21] The hack exposed confidential email correspondence between Soros and Ukrainian President Petro Poroshenko. In one email, Soros laid out a strategy for Ukraine to obtain a much-needed $15 billion in financial support from the European Union (EU). He concluded the email as follows,

> Based on that commitment, the Federal Reserve could be asked to extend a $15 billion three-month swap arrangement with the National Bank of Ukraine. That would reassure the markets and avoid a panic. . .. If you do, you would have to call Chancellor Merkel to ask for a commitment in principle to the $15 billion package. I am ready to call Jack Lew of the US Treasury to sound him out about the swap agreement.[22]

Call Jack Lew? Since when does a businessman call the U.S. Treasury for funds to support a foreign country, even if it is an ally? Such actions beg the question, "how did Soros have that kind of influence?" Maybe because he was bankrolling Obama's presidency in hopes that Obama would further his European vision expressed during a ValueWalks speech?[23]

> "The European Union was a very inspiring idea to people like me." Reflecting back to when European economies were more balanced, "It was the embodiment of the concept of an Open Society, like-minded countries getting together and sacrificing part of their sovereignty for the common good. It was meant to be a voluntary association of equals.[24]

It's important to note the term "Open Society" in Soros' speech. There is a direct connection between this term and his vision, as represented by his philanthropic organization, *the Open Society Foundation.*

The Open Society Foundation (OSF) is a U.S.-based humanitarian NGO with far-reaching implications—as seen with MoveOn.org. Furthermore, OSF has close ties with U.S. Institutions such as USAID.

According to Global Research,

USAID, working with billionaire George Soros' Open Society, also funds the Organized Crime and Corruption

Reporting Project, which engages in 'investigative journalism' that usually goes after governments that have fallen into disfavor with the United States and then are singled out for accusations of corruption. The USAID-funded OCCRP collaborates with Bellingcat, an online investigative website founded by blogger Eliot Higgins.[25]

OSF also uses incitement to further its "so-called" social justice agendas. For example, it is well-known that George Soros, through the Open Society Foundation, funded a base of activist groups to mobilize the Ferguson protests. How much did he donate? Thirty-three million dollars. And this is social justice? According to the Daily Mail, "Liberal billionaire George Soros donated $33 million to social justice organizations which helped turn events in Ferguson from a local protest into a national flashpoint."[26]

In the words of the Washington Times,

"Its liberal billionaire George Soros, who has built a business empire that dominates across the ocean in Europe while forging a political machine powered by nonprofit foundations that impact American politics and policy, not unlike what he did with MoveOn.org." And "Mr. Soros gave at least $33 million in one year to support already-established groups that emboldened the grass-roots, on-the-ground activists in Ferguson, according to the most recent tax filings of his nonprofit Open Society Foundations."[27]

In summary, George Soros used the Ferguson shooting to turn a "one-day criminal event in Missouri into a 24-hour-a-day national cause for celebration."[28] Tell me, how did this help the Ferguson community? How did this work towards justice on behalf of Michael Brown or Officer Darren Wilson? And how has it fostered reconciliation and peace-making on any level?

What is truly sad is that Mr. Soros and his Open Society Foundation are not furthering a better America. Instead, they inject the viper's venom into American Society by trashing American justice and constitutional values while playing the human rights social justice race card.

Today, social justice trends that equate "race and color to everything just" are fomented in America. Hence, if a minority (legal or illegal) commits a crime or assaults, a police officer is viewed as the "just" victim, and the non-minority citizen (regardless of race) is looked upon as the "unjust" perpetrator. No more is breaking the law regarded as breaking the law. It is propagandized with a racial bias that says, "if a minority is arrested for a crime, it is because the majority community is racist." In most cases, <u>nothing</u> could be farther from the truth.

Therefore, it's important to clarify that "being a minority is not a crime, but breaking the law is."

No moral equivalence exists between a minority breaking the law and a white majority. However, there is a moral distinction between being a minority and breaking the law. This difference must not be distorted by any sect of American society, including government elites.

Unethical and illegal behavior must remain the demarcation line for justice and judgment. This does not mean that every crime deserves a jail sentence or a punishment. Still, we must remain vigilant to uphold justice by calling out bad moral behavior and rewarding good moral behavior; no more blurring the lines. If, as a nation, Americans choose not to be law-abiding citizens, what Isaiah said about "justice and judgment being turned back" will become the ethos of a lawless America. Historically, there is only one action that could change this trend. "Teshuva,[29] repentance"—doing an about-face and returning to God, who is the author of just human rights laws; the basis of Constitutional America. Consider the city of Nineveh as a precedence.

With that said, I would be remiss not to mention that George Soros was behind the Panama Papers scandal of leaked documents released on April 3, 2016, by the German newspaper Süddeutsche Zeitung (SZ), dubbing them the "Panama Papers." The papers exposed the network of more than 214,000 tax havens involving people and entities from 200 different nations.[30]

Behind the investigation and leak of the Panama Papers scandal was The International Consortium of Investigative Journalists (ICIJ). An organization funded by none other than George Soros and the Open Society Foundation.

About the ICIJ, you might find the following statement of interest:

> The United States Center for Public Integrity and the International Consortium of Investigative Journalists participated in a multi-year media war, which Soros launched against the Koch brothers, billionaires associated with right-wing Republican circles. Periodically, during the campaign, Soros' journalists were convicted of outright fraud, violating U.S. law, and distorting facts.[31]

Another player in the Panama Papers leak was the Ford Foundation. According to Hang The Bankers, "The Ford Foundation is connected to the CIA and has specialized in international cultural propaganda since the end of the Second World War." Henry Ford was also involved in Nazi propaganda in the United States during World War II. He even received the *Adolf Hitler Award*. Did you know Ford was honored by the Nazis?

In 2016, I sat with the author of the May 2016 NGO Monitor's UNOCHA-oPt (United Nations Office for the Coordination of Humanitarian Affairs) report. The report's findings revealed extensive data manipulation by the UN to delegitimize Israel. The document mentions numerous NGOs (non-governmental organizations) and their acts to delegitimize Israel. While discussing the findings with the author, she highlighted the Ford Foundation's involvement. This insight later revealed that the Ford Foundation and the Open Society Foundation, directly and indirectly, fund most anti-Israel NGOs.

With that said, the Panama Papers leak had a geopolitical agenda. All the elites mentioned in the scandal, of which Vladimir Putin was at the top, are not only the opponents of George Soros but also the geopolitical enemies of the U.S. State Department.[32] According to the editor of the Event Chronicles,

> The offshore scandal is the result of a public-private partnership. All persons involved are Soros' opponents, but when they are also the geopolitical enemies of the U.S., the most serious charges are put forward. . .. Liberal left figures associated with Soros himself, who actively use offshore companies for financial speculation, do not appear anywhere on the lists.[33]

The Panama Paper scandal leads us right back to where we started: George Soros' connection to the U.S. Treasury and other governmental organizations, including but not limited to the CIA and the U.S. State Department.

By August of 2010, there were reports that Soros had allegedly visited the White House 35 times.[34][35] He not only met with President Obama but also with a man named Rob Malley.

Who is Rob Malley? Robert Malley was a special assistant to President Obama on the National Security Council (NSC), a senior advisor to the president for the counter-ISIL campaign, and the White House coordinator for the Middle East, North Africa, and the Persian Gulf region.[36] He was often referred to as Obama's ISIL Czar.

But before becoming a senior National Security Advisor, he served as the Middle East and North Africa Program Director of the Soros-funded International Crisis Group.[37] Furthermore, Malley's fascinating family background has undoubtedly created some strong anti-democratic pro-Marxist biases. Notably, his family is vehemently anti-Israel and boasts of being good friends with Yasser Arafat.[38] That makes sense when you learn that his parents started the Egyptian Communist Party and later were kicked out of France for their radical views and threats to chiefs of state. What's that adage, "Birds of a feather flock together?"

Are you beginning to see how deep this Washington web goes and how many cockatrice eggs are lying around? Are you starting to see what and who Donald Trump was against during his 2016 election? And why that every time he mentioned a problem within Washington, he stepped on a cockatrice egg, and out came a viper?

I'm almost done talking about Soros. Do you have any questions? Would you like to know how much money he poured into Hillary's campaign? Or how he manipulates European election outcomes? What about his organization's active role in Ukraine?

As for Hillary, the documented figures show that Soros donated over 8 million to her campaign[39] and over 25 million to Democratic candidates. In addition to Hillary, her running mate Senator Tim Kaine held a private dinner with Soros' son, Alexander—another top-tier financier of the Democratic party. DC Leaks exposed Soros for using his NGOs to manipulate European elections.[40]

Thankfully, Soros and his money couldn't buy the American people in the 2016 election—however, the jury is still out for the 2020 election.

As we segue into chapter two to discuss issues behind Trump's campaign that clashed with the Washington Web, let me share one last thing about George Soros—he has an acute messianic complex.

In 2004, the L.A. Times penned the following:

"America, under Bush, is a danger to the world," says Soros.

To save the world and prevent the reelection of George W. Bush, Soros has dedicated extraordinary amounts of time and money because defeating Bush, he says, is his "central focus." His motto, "If I spend enough, I will make it right," is the essence of his articulated ideas about changing society. "I do not accept the rules imposed by others. . ..

And in periods of regime change, the normal rules don't apply. . .. "

"If truth be known, I carried some rather potent messianic fantasies with me from childhood, which I felt I had to control; otherwise, they might get me in trouble. . .. Next to my fantasies about being God, I also have very strong fantasies of being mad," Soros once confided on British television.[41]

Throughout the election campaign, I wondered if Hillary wasn't Soros' proxy and it was Soros running against Trump—two Billionaires dueling it out for America's soul being suffocated by illegal immigration, unprotected borders, and rabid corruption.

Who knew that when Trump called out illegal immigration, unprotected borders, and a corrupt Mexican Government, he would step on not just one cockatrice egg but a whole nest! And inevitably, out came the adders and the vipers striking with precision and recoiling as if nothing happened.

Was Trump's position statement on Mexico and immigration a valid issue for his campaign? Was this as big of a problem as he insisted it was? And if so, what solutions did Donald Trump provide for America?

Let's find out.

CHAPTER TWO

Legal or Illegal?

"One law shall be to him that is home born, and unto the stranger that sojourns among you." Exodus 12:49

෨

As Americans, whether conservative or liberal, immigration is at the heart of who we are—a nation of immigrants. Whether it's our founding fathers who sought freedom from religious oppression and tyranny or our masses who fled Europe pre-and post-Holocaust, or our Mexican and South American immigrants escaping poverty, or our Syrian refugees escaping death, one thing is forever settled in the American collective conscience—they are welcome in America.

For the world, America is a place of hope, a place where their world can change and where they can change the world. So, what's the problem?

For over a decade, government policies have given rise to serious immigration issues, of which the word "illegal" is center stage.

And although illegal immigration has been at the forefront of political debates, it was not until Donald Trump linked Mexico and Mexicans with "crime, drug cartels, rape and murder" that the whole discussion erupted into a violent mass media race-bashing frenzy.

On June 16th, 2015, when Mr. Trump announced his run for President, he also highlighted the issues that would be addressed in his candidacy—and at the top was the cockatrice egg: Illegal Immigration. And when he stepped on it—out came a viper.

Here is an excerpt from his speech:

When do we beat Mexico at the border? They're laughing at us, at our stupidity. And now they are beating us economically. They are not our friends, believe me. But they're killing us economically. The U.S. has become a dumping ground for everybody else's problems. (Applause)

Thank you. It's true, and these are the best and the finest. When Mexico sends its people, they're not sending their best. They're not sending you. They're not sending you. They're sending people that have lots of problems, and they're bringing those problems with them. They're bringing drugs. They're bringing crime. They're rapists. And some, I assume, are good people. But I speak to border guards, and they tell us what we're getting. And it only makes common sense. It only makes common sense. They're not sending us the right people.

It's coming from more than Mexico. It's coming from all over South and Latin America, and it's coming probably — probably — from the Middle East. But we don't know. Because we have no protection and we have no competence, we don't know what's happening. And it's got to stop, and it's got to stop fast.

Notably, weeks after Donald Trump's scathing assessment of how the Mexican government was sending murderers and rapists, Kate Steinle, a thirty-two-year-old woman, was murdered by an illegal Mexican immigrant, Juan Francisco Lopez-Sanchez, on San Francisco Pier 14, in July of 2015.

Bill O'Reilly took the killing of Kate Steinle very seriously and tied it into his Talking Points Memo entitled, "The Vilification of Donald Trump."

He pointed out that Donald Trump was correct in his assessment of the border situation but could have been more articulate and precise in the way he portrayed Mexico and Mexican illegals—because, he said, most illegals are good law-abiding citizens, not murderers and rapists (of which I wholeheartedly agree).

In his Talking Points Memo, he referred to the 1996 "Illegal Immigration Reform and Responsibility Act (IIRIRA)" that Bill Clinton signed into law. This act made it clear that "local and state authorities were to cooperate with the

Federal Government in apprehending illegals, especially illegal criminals." Time and time again, illegal criminals were given a pass and often found living in Sanctuary cities that would not deport or imprison them.

Concerning Kate Steinle, O'Reilly rightly condemned the establishment's response to San Francisco's violation of the law and noted, "Racial politics drives the law these days, which is why Trump caught so much hell. The Constitution demands that the Federal Government protects the American people from foreign intruders; it demands it." He continues, "Obviously, that responsibility is not being met. But if you point that out, as Mr. Trump did, you are a racist. A piñata for the border crowd to bash."

Bill O'Reilly acted and developed Kate's Law. How did the Latino community respond to that?

Samanta Honigman, an undergraduate student at New York University, wrote the following in her article, "Kate's Law and the License to Hate."[42]

"Kate's Law" addresses what is really a bureaucratic problem with a nuclear bomb. Sections of "Kate's Law" actually create stricter punishments, a legal double standard, for all undocumented immigrants. In fact, as you can see from page 3 on BillCam, the bill gives people without papers much harsher sentences for the same offense than someone with papers would receive. Surely this violates the section of the 14th Amendment that ensures the due process of law for all persons, regardless of immigration status.

If that doesn't make you want to pull your hair out, I don't know what does. She just said, "an illegal immigrant has the same rights as a legal immigrant and, therefore, has a right to due process of law."

When I worked for Jewish Vocational Services, I taught immigrants and underprivileged women office skills for placement in the workplace. To thwart specific unethical actions, I put up a sign spanning the top of my entire blackboard; it read, "what don't you understand about the word, NO?" Today, the banner would read, "what don't you understand about the word ILLEGAL?"

With that said, as Americans, we need leadership to revamp and streamline the U.S. immigration process, not abrogate it. We need new laws, a legal system that facilitates citizenship for those who are vetted, and legislation that helps vet those who are illegal. We need to permanently deport all illegals who commit crimes. We should not spend one more dollar holding them in our Prisons. Furthermore, we should make it clear to every foreign government that if we catch one of your citizens committing a crime in our country—they will be deported, and you will pay all fees, including the airfare for their deportation. And, as noted, they should never be allowed back into our country. Why? Because they did not respect the opportunity availed to them. And because deterrence is the best way to minimize crime, illegal immigration, and terrorism.

This brings us to the issue of "entitlement."

∾

Entitled or Entitlement?

Under the Obama administration, there was an ideological shift in how Americans think. The tenets of the European Union, the United Nations Human Rights Council, decentralized market globalization, increased government handouts, and the blurring of all moral lines have sadly given way to an "entitlement" mentality within our society.

This sense of "entitlement" made its way into the immigration narrative, particularly among those who migrated from South American, Mexican, and Muslim societies. During the Obama and now the Biden administration, entitlement philosophy has burgeoned within all economic and social classes. Instead of immigrants legally striving for the American Dream, social justice movements have encouraged illegal immigrants to reach for American entitlement—a lawless, unethical and destructive ideal that rewards illegals and punishes hard-working American citizens.

California is one of the most emotionally broken and financially bankrupt states in the U.S. It no longer distinguishes between illegal and legal. Every illegal can obtain a Driver's License and voter registration card—are you ok with that?

If you pay attention to the radical legislation Governor Newsom has passed, you would see on the docket the legalization of <u>human composting</u> as a new burial option for

Californians.[43] Yes, you read it right, Human composting—the same process used to make fertilizer from your vegetable scraps. Devaluing human life is one of the first steps to genocide. And it all begins with removing human dignity—an attribute that comes with legal citizenship, not entitlement.

Obama's idea of entitlement was that illegal immigrants or refugees are "entitled" to all our benefits without having to "obey" any of our laws. And, if you don't like one of our laws, as in the case of the Secure Communities and IIRIRA, we will either change them or get rid of them for you.

Former President Obama lived in Eurotopia. What is Eurotopia? It is an elite humanitarian utopia that exists without the constraints of moral law. It compels American leaders and citizens alike to dispense with accountability, secure borders, the Constitution, the American dream, and above all, "justice and judgment." It invites the U.S. to join the human rights cesspool of tolerance, hypocrisy, immoral equivalence, injustice, and an over-regulated European Union. Yes, that is Eurotopia, an elite humanitarian utopia.

If you think that is an exaggeration, keep reading.

Illegal immigrants have come to believe that it is not illegal to be illegal. They feel that if their country is suffering economically, experiencing gang violence, or being oppressed by a ruthless dictator, then it is our responsibility to help them. And the process of becoming a legal immigrant is, well, just too difficult.

According to Samanta Honigman,

Few of us would wait for the United States to process a visa over the course of many years if our families just over the border were in continual danger. One might ask, "why can't Latino immigrants simply go through the process of securing citizenship?" But few understand that applying for permanent residence and citizenship is a timely, expensive and arduous process, and it is out of reach for those who suffer the most economically. Sometimes, decent people feel that there is no other option but to live under the radar, at least for a while.

Very few people do understand Samanta why you and some in the Latino community feel that our process of immigration is "out of reach" for your human rights problems. And this was precisely what Trump was driving at—equity for legal American citizens does not include entitlement for illegal-American citizens.

So, how did "entitlement" become part of our immigrant "belief system?"

Let's return to the 1996 "Illegal Immigration Reform and Responsibility Act (IIRIRA)"—the hidden part.

The 1996 IIRIRA was a framework for establishing a national identification system for Americans. The structure consisted of three Identification systems offered to states as "test pilots." The provision provided grants of $5 million per year to any State participating in one of three pilot ID programs.

You may ask, why would that be important to our discussion on immigration? Because one of those programs was the "Criminal Alien Identification Program." This ID program was to link the fingerprint records of previously arrested aliens with federal, state, and local law enforcement agencies.

ဢ

Secure Communities to the Dream Act

Fast forward to 2009, the program became known as Secure Communities.[44] It was managed by the U.S. Immigration and Customs Enforcement (ICE), Interior Immigration, and the Department of Homeland Security. Julia Preston wrote in her New York Times article dated November 12, 2009, that the Federal authorities had identified more than 111,000 immigrants with criminal records:

> Among the immigrants identified through the program, known as Secure Communities, more than 111,000 had been charged with or convicted of the most severe crimes, including murder and rape, domestic security officials said Thursday. About 1,900 of those were deported.

> She stated that "about 100,000 detained immigrants identified through the system had been convicted of less serious crimes, ranging from burglary to traffic offenses."

> John Morton of ICE stated that Secure Communities were "the future of immigration enforcement" because it "focuses

our resources on identifying and removing the most serious criminal offenders first and foremost."[45]

The goals of Secure Communities, as outlined in a 2009 report to Congress, were to Identify, Prioritize, and Transform (IPT). *Identify* criminal aliens through modernized information sharing; *Prioritize* enforcement actions to ensure apprehension and removal of dangerous illegal aliens; and *Transform* criminal alien enforcement processes and systems to achieve lasting results."[46]

Wow! You can go ahead and say it! Since 2009 "we've come a long way, baby!" Did immigration crime rates drop significantly since Secure Communities were expanded under the previous Obama administration?

Before we continue discussing what happened with Secure Communities, let's take note of some facts in Julia's article. First, in 2008 over 111,000 illegal immigrants were charged with serious crimes, including murder and rape! Secondly, over 100,000 have committed minor crimes like burglary. Sound familiar?

When Donald Trump said that the crimes committed by illegals ranged from theft to rape, was he lying? Was he exaggerating? What do you think? Do you think rape is a serious crime? And how dangerous is burglary?

President Trump believed these crimes were severe and subject to the statutes of law. However, under the current administration, the threat level of a crime is not based on the laws of justice but on human rights.

The Secure Communities project underwent several transitions between 2009 and 2012 until it was finally abandoned in 2014. Most of the changes occurred between 2011 and 2012, before Obama's re-election. He wanted the Latino vote, and to obtain it, he reneged and dissolved policies that directly affected the security of the American people.

In 2012, the Congressional Hispanic Caucus requested the suspension of the deportation program because they found it to be based on "administrative authority only." Subsequently, Boston Mayor Thomas Menino reported that "the program, contrary to its stated goal, is negatively impacting public safety," and numerous immigrants have been deported after committing only minor traffic violations.[47] Of those deported from Illinois through May 2011, by ICE's accounting, less than 22% were convicted of a severe crime, 75% were never convicted of a serious crime, and more than 21% were not convicted of any offense.

Furthermore, the AFL-CIO, an organization representing 7,000 ICE officers, issued a no-confidence vote due to the discrepancy in the documentation. The ICE officers noted that the number of non-criminal ICE deportees was highly overinflated, stating that "many offenders agreed to be deported if all charges were dropped and they returned to the category of non-criminal."[4849] Also, the ICE internal reports revealed that local authorities arrested 90% of all ICE detainees, yet the public report showed otherwise.[50] That was just part of their accusations. According to Chris Crane, President of the National ICE Council Union, who testified before Congress, "the government was ordering the agents not to enforce the law to comply with the President's re-election campaign priorities.[5152]

Hence, enters the Dream Act—Obama's answer to the then "highly controversial" Security Communities. It is important to note that Security Communities became highly criticized by local authorities due to the additional costs of implementing the 48-hour detainee rule. Furthermore, State and local officials felt it was wrong to deport illegal immigrants with minor criminal infractions or no criminal record—this thinking deserves a station identification break. Since when are "illegal" immigrants defined by whether or not they committed a crime?

§

The Dream Act

The Dream Act was enacted to repair damaged relations between President Obama and Latino voters. So, what exactly was the Dream Act offering?

For starters, "prosecutorial discretion." Prosecutorial discretion meant that reviews were done on a case-by-case basis. Once reviewed, Secretary Napolitano would provide relief for the accused. Individuals who qualified for aid could also be granted work permits. Furthermore, the new policy made deportation cases involving people with no significant criminal record less likely.[5354] Napolitano, who resigned in 2013, said that the administration's policy "will not alleviate the need for passage of the Dream Act or larger reforms to our immigration laws."

By summer 2011, according to Dino Grandoni of The Atlantic Wire, Obama had reportedly deported 1,000,000 illegal Mexicans. But by the summer of 2012, deportations had trickled to a slow drip, and by 2013 President Obama was making deals with the Mexican[55] and South American governments to ensure free passage, education, and welfare to illegals who cross our southern American borders.[56]

In November 2015, the Pew report published their annual "5 Facts About Illegal Immigration in the U.S."[57] The five facts included an explanation of Obama's expanded deportation relief which the Supreme Court voted down on June 23, 2016. The Pew report noted that, in 2014, there were 11.3 million illegal immigrants in America, making up 3-5% of our population. Of those 11.3 million, Mexican illegal immigrants made up 49%, collectively accounting for over 5% of the American workforce. And sadly, 7% of students K-12 in our public schools have at least one illegal parent. These statistics are not only daunting, but they reaffirm the need for a reformed immigration process—and quickly.

Unfortunately, daunting turned into nightmarish by the minute. On June 29, 2016, President Obama met with Mexican President Nieto and Canadian Prime Minister Trudeau to discuss the Trans-Pacific Trade Agreement. You may recall earlier in the chapter that I mentioned Obama had a Eurotopia vision for America and the world. At the center of the "trifecta amigo meeting" was the idea of "no borders" between our countries—just like Europe. Let's be one big happy trade family. No borders. Your problems are my problems!

Of course, Trump was central to the discussions, and thankfully, neither Nieto nor Trudeau was foolish enough to fall for Obama's bait. They sidestepped specific questions about Trump, saying they would gladly work with whoever was elected to lead the United States.

But Obama wasn't happy with their graceful evasion of condemning Trump. He pushed the immigration agenda saying, "whoever becomes president of the United States is going to have a deep, strong interest in having a strong relationship with Mexico. That's our neighbor, our friend, and one of our biggest trading partners. I think I've made myself clear, setting aside whatever the candidates say, that America is a nation of immigrants; that's our strength."

Wait for it . . ..

"Unless you were one of the first Americans unless you are Native American, somebody, somewhere, in your past showed up from someplace else. And they didn't always have papers."[58]

Need I say more? Yes.

℘

Arizona's Conundrum

To continue the subject of immigration after what seems to be the perfect ending to this chapter may seem a little excessive. So, if you need to take a five-minute break—do it now. As Paul Harvey would say, "Now, for the rest of the story."

You may remember the 2012 Supreme Court's ruling on Arizona's Immigration Laws.

There was a split decision by the Supreme Court, and the last three clauses were deemed unconstitutional. They revoked Arizona's right to criminally penalize persons for seeking work or failing to register with the federal government. They stopped police from making warrantless arrests based upon suspicion of suspected illegal status and deportation ability under federal law. And they ensured that immigrants would not be required to carry national proof of their legal status.[59]

The only clause that remained was the "show me your papers" provision, which allowed state law enforcement officials to check the immigration status of a person who was stopped or arrested, and only if they had reason to suspect them of being in the country illegally.[60]

While attending the University of Haifa, I wrote the first edition of this book. While living in Haifa, I often traveled from Haifa to Tel Aviv or Jerusalem to stay with friends over Shabbat (Friday evening to Saturday night). As I approached the train station with my tiny overnight bag, I was asked, in Hebrew, for my identification. I had to show the Security Guard my U.S. Passport, or I could not travel—it was that simple. And that's within the country; I am not even crossing a border! Yet, in my own country, law enforcement is forbidden to check a foreigner's identification. Members of drug cartels and terrorist networks, along with law-abiding citizens, can cross state lines and set up shop; nobody is the wiser. And some think Trump is too vocal about this issue. Now that you have more facts, what do you think?

Regarding Arizona state law, the final statement made by the Supreme Court was "The State may not pursue policies that undermine Federal Law," and "detaining individuals solely to verify their immigration status would raise constitutional concerns," wrote Justice Anthony Kennedy, expressing the majority opinion. Justice Antonin Scalia, of blessed memory, vocally objected to the majority argument in this case and the administration's immigration policies.[61]

When Obama took office in 2012, the 1996 "Illegal Immigration Reform and Responsibility Act (IIRIRA)" was dismantled. All immigration restrictions marginalized and security protocols minimized—all in the name of "affirmative action" and "liberty."

And as for making an example out of Arizona? Then President Obama expressed his fear that the ONE provision accepted by the court may lead to racial profiling.[62] So let's go there.

෫ා

What's Racial Profiling?

What is racial profiling? Why did President Obama hate it so much? How could it be used to keep Americans safe? And why did Trump consider it?

These are just a few questions that play a significant role in understanding how and why our National Security entities—from NSA to TSA struggle to be effective.

In 1968, my mother put me on a plane all by myself. I was eight years old when I received my first Bronze Wings from the Delta stewardess assigned to oversee me. That was many years ago. Since then, I've been privileged to fly around the world, literally. I love to travel and explore this magnificent world God created for us. The world is full of beautiful people, rich and diverse cultures, spectacular scenery, life-giving wildernesses, and very cool animals.

But travel has changed, *really* changed since I was a little girl. Oh, how I loved the Delta Wings I received from the flight attendants. And when it came to meals, which were included on even shorter flights, it was enchanting to receive a meal tray with a quaint place setting with a china plate, vintage petite silverware, and a teacup. Believe it or not, I still have my Finnish Air silverware from my first overseas flight from Chicago to the Soviet Union in 1977. And might I add, security was a breeze. No need to take off your shoes or belts—remember? Why? It was not because there were no threats or we were too lax. It was simply because, at that time, we profiled; yep, National Security included profiling.

After 9/11, all that changed. Heightened security scares and political attempts to abate attacks on innocent Muslim citizens wrought dramatic security changes. It started with shoes, and it evolved into X-ray machines. I lived in Singapore during 9/11 and remembered returning to a different America.

Today, many of us only have beautiful memories of how "it used to be."

I traveled in and out of Israel for over ten years before 9/11. And, let me tell you, going through Israeli security was no picnic. You never saw anyone mistreated, just intensely questioned. No removal of shoes or belts—but they checked your suitcase. Even though it took time, it was efficient and effective. You felt safe when you boarded or exited the plane. I did not live under any false illusions during those years. On at least two occasions during my stay in Israel, just a few minutes made the difference between life and death.

I am pointing this out because after the government introduced TSA into our lives, traveling in and out of America became a nightmare. A new branch of the U.S. Government became responsible for our National Security which included catching the bad guys in airports—except they forgot that 99% of Americans were not the "bad guys." After the Bush and subsequent Obama administrations had gotten rid of profiling, everyone became a suspect.

I've often compared security systems between the two countries and vocally made my observations known when frustrated—not good. Israel profiles. In Israel, you'll see men and women taken to the side and interrogated before entering security lines. You'll see questionable characters pulled out of the line or asked to step aside when it is their turn to be questioned. And because Israel profiles, threats are quickly averted, so everyday travelers are not subject to unnecessary interrogation, search, or seizure.

In Israel, your initial interview with the security team is part of profiling. After being interviewed, you and your luggage are given a number ranging from 1 to 6. If you receive a six, you are a very high-security risk. Israeli security will manually search all your bags with a high-tech scanning system. And, if available, you will be sent to the body scanner and get your complimentary security massage. The number 6 is not just relegated to suspected terrorists. You may be an American citizen who travels to other Middle Eastern countries, many of which do not have relations with Israel. Or you may make frequent trips to Asia, including Malaysia and Indonesia. If so, you will receive a higher number and be subject to more stringent security measures, including character profiling consisting of behavioral and pattern profiling. Israel's HUMINT (human intelligence) is well trained to recognize it.

There is no replacement for profiling. Sadly, profiling has become a racial term—yet, it has little to do with "racism."

So, if not racism, what is profiling? And why is it essential to National Security?

According to dictionary.com, profiling is "the use of personal characteristics or behavior patterns to determine whether a person may be engaged in illegal activity."

Does that sound like racism to you?

No, because profiling is not confined to a specific race, nor is it singling out a race for vindictive reasons—it is looking for behavior patterns that can potentially lead to danger. In a sense, we are not profiling race; we are profiling evil. We are looking for criminals, drug cartels, fraud rings, thieves, smugglers, arms distributors, terrorists, and the like. Unfortunately, many of those categories exist within specific minority communities.

Take the Boston Bombers, for example—they were of Russian origin and Muslim. In 2011, the FBI was informed by the FSB (Russian Federal Security Service) that Tamerlan, one of the bombers, had become a "radical follower of Islam."[63] In 2012 he traveled to Chechnya and attended a mosque known for its radical ties. Once again, the FSB warned the FBI, yet it turned a blind eye. Tamerlan returned to America without any security checks. The FBI's "turn a blind eye we can't profile" approach resulted in three dead and 264 injured Americans.

It is imperative to understand security through the looking glass of good and evil, right and wrong, moral and immoral—not race or culture. Terrorism is an evil act committed against people, precious people.

So why was President Obama so averse to profiling? Could it be because his political interests and affiliations with terrorist organizations had blinded his ability to discern between National Security and the placating of minority and human rights groups? Or did the political makeup of his staff members intervene with our National Security interests?

Regrettably, profiling has become a human rights issue. And the problem often lies with organizations that support human rights activism. These groups twist Constitutional laws to make judges, lawyers, and civilians believe that profiling violates human rights and is, therefore, racist.

Do you think the U.S. should be more involved with profiling? Could profiling improve our National Security? Let's turn to President Donald Trump to find out what he believes about profiling.

৪৩

Trump Profile?

On June 19, 2016, Trump told CBS, "Well, I think profiling is something that we're going to have to start thinking about as a country; other countries do it; you look at Israel, and you look at others, and they do it, and they do it successfully. You know, I hate the concept of profiling. But we have to start using common sense."

His speech came after the mass shooting in Orlando, Florida, where 49 people were left dead and 40 others injured after a radicalized Muslim opened fire at an LGBT bar. Admittedly, this was not the only terrorist attack on our soil. We have witnessed two on U.S. Army bases, as was the case twice at Ft. Hood. And since the Obama administration did not want to label them terrorist attacks, the means and methods of deterring them were not utilized.

In a discussion on the deterrence of terrorism, Donald Trump referred to the New York Police Department's Demographics Unit, which used various means of surveillance on the Muslim communities and Mosques to keep tabs on any uptick in radical behavior. After Bill de Blasio had become Mayor, the program was dismantled.

According to the AP-GfK poll conducted from March 31 through April 4, 2016, "49% of respondents said that they 'favored surveillance programs aimed at predominantly Muslim communities in the United States to obtain information about possible radicalization.' 47% opposed surveillance."

Of course, civil libertarians, Muslims, and others strongly oppose the idea of profiling, arguing that it is unconstitutional and discriminatory based on race, religion, and other factors.[64] New York has had to settle two lawsuits linked to surveillance. Suppose President Trump and Congress allowed a profiling system to become part of our National Security program. In that case, he would face opposition from these communities while attempting to institute its benefits.

Sadly, while updating this book, a terrorist attack struck the heart of New York.[65] Eight lives were snuffed out by an ISIS terrorist, Sayfullo Saipov,[66] just a few blocks from the World Trade Center Memorial. Why? Firstly, because of the Diversity Visa (no vetting) Lottery Program initiated by New York's own Senator Chuck Schumer—he traded security for merit. Secondly, no surveillance. According to NJ.com, "The backyard of Saipov's apartment complex abuts the Masjid Omar Mosque, where many in the community visit each day for prayer services. The NYPD targeted the mosque in 2006 in a controversial surveillance program."[67] Sadly, that wasn't the case in 2017.

Trump nailed this issue during his campaign, and as President, he attempted to bring about the change necessary for all American citizens' safety—including Muslims. Did you know that radical Islam kills its own when they do not adhere to its extreme ideology?

೭ට

The Great Wall

Lastly, in our discussion on immigration, we must visit the great wall Mexico was going to finance.

Amidst the pro and con Trump sentiments, there was among certain media outlets a consensus that Trump was inconsistent and wishy-washy over policy. One of the common rebuttals about Trump is that "he had no consistent policy."

The truth is that Trump's policies were far more consistent than the media wanted to admit. And, to be fair, until he took office, he was a Washington outsider. Meaning he followed his experience and gut on what's right and what's wrong with our country while learning, along the way, how to develop position statements that were feasible within the context of existing laws and policies. Not an easy task. So, during his campaign, most conservative Americans cut him a lot of slack when he rubbed people the wrong way over issues.

With that said, many of his position statements, including that on border control and the Wall, were available on his website www.donaldjtrump.com. We will discuss the position statement, "Compelling Mexico to Pay for the Wall."[68] If you had the opportunity to read it, it was exceptionally written. Let me summarize it for you.

Trump saw our border problem and Mexico's infringement of American sovereignty as a breach of the Patriot Act. The USA Patriot Act was established to "deter and punish terrorist acts in the United States and around the world, to enhance law enforcement investigatory tools, and other purposes."[69] Such deterrence deals with international money laundering, the financing of terrorism, the scrutiny of a foreign jurisdiction, foreign financial institutions, and classes of international transactions subject to criminal abuse. It requires financial services to report potential money laundering, prevent the use of the U.S. financial system for personal gain by corrupt foreign officials, and facilitate the repatriation of stolen assets to the citizens of countries to which such assets belong.

Section 326, *Verification of Identification,* "prescribes regulations establishing minimum standards for financial institutions and their customers regarding the identity of a client that shall apply to the opening of an account at the financial institution."

In President Trump's words, it is the "know your customer" provision, compelling financial institutions to demand identity documents before opening accounts or conducting financial transactions. Detailed regulations of section 326 are found at 31 CFR 130.120-121.

And because of the Patriot Act section 326 and several other sections, paying for the wall would have been an easy decision for Mexico. Mexico could have made a one-time payment of $5-10 billion to the United States Treasury. In turn, she would ensure that $24 billion in aid continues to flow into the country yearly. What's interesting is how Mr. Trump used the Patriot Act to compel Mexico to finance the wall and how he intended to implement his plan—day by day.

It's too unique not to include in the book:

Day 1: He planned to promulgate a "proposed rule" to amend 31 CFR 130.121. It would aim to "redefine applicable financial institutions to include money transfer companies like the Western Union and to redefine "account" to include wire transfers. More importantly, it would include a "requirement that no alien may wire money outside of the United States unless the alien first provides a document establishing his lawful presence in the United States."

Day 2: He stated that Mexico would protest. Here, we learn how the $24 billion was to be remitted to Mexico via Mexican Nationals working in the United States, of which the majority were illegal (well, at least 49%, as noted in the Pew report).

Day 3: Mexico was told that if they financed the wall, the Trump Administration would not promulgate the final rule, and the regulation would not go into effect.

Trump further explained how using Trade Tariffs and enforcing existing Trade Rules would offset losses to the U.S. caused by Mexico's unethical subsidy behavior. In turn, it would provide income gains that would finance the wall. He also talked about "leveraging visas." Canceling visas is an option. Trump said, "Immigration is a privilege, not a right," and Mexico depends on the United States as a "release valve" for its poverty. We approve hundreds of thousands of visas annually, and by adding a slight increase to the cost, we could pay for the wall.

The seriousness with which Trump contemplated the facts and leveraged options regarding Mexico's financing of a system for secure borders reveals that Trump had American interests at heart, disliked inequity, and knew the steps necessary to correct the problem. He was intent on securing our borders and thought through how and why Mexico should aid in paying for the wall.

While President, he took action. By September 2017, eight prototypes were being built across the southern border. Congress funded the prototypes, and ultimately, one was chosen for the wall.[70]

Very few leaders are willing to take a politically incorrect stand on issues vital to America's national interests. Scripture speaks about the neighbor who is not equitable. And when he is found out, part of his civic responsibility is to make reparations commensurate up to seven times that he has unjustly taken.

The wisdom of Trump's immigration proposals and strategies was intended to be restorative while improving our immigration process. Just think, if Trump were successful, immigrants would no longer have to hide in the shadows of society. They wouldn't have to risk their lives to come to America. Nor would you have the current catastrophic problem at the borders. Trump's immigration views were postured to move us one step closer to making America Great Again.

ॐ

Turning the Tide

In closing, it's important to reiterate that the political divide in our country over foreign immigrants has never been about immigrants per se but "illegal" immigrants. And all the brouhaha over Donald Trump's Mexican wall brought some very positive trends to the immigration crisis during his Presidency.

According to Attorney and Professor Allan Wernick (Baruch College), who runs the immigration legal services program at CUNY and writes a twice-weekly immigration column in the Daily News,

> We expect that there's going to be an increased number of people who want to be U.S. citizens. The anti-immigration rhetoric that has driven some candidates' campaigns is leading many immigrants to become citizens, not only so that they can vote but so that they are protected if the strict policies candidates like Donald Trump have touted are enacted.[71]

All the bad press was producing something good—legal immigration. Amazing how easy the "path to citizenship" can be when excuses and unnecessary obstacles are removed.

Entire volumes can be written about the past, present, and future challenges of America's immigration system. I have only touched on a few issues in the forefront because of Donald Trump's nomination and subsequent Presidential victory.

If you are an immigrant reading this book or a second-generation immigrant, of which I am, or a third or a fourth—I want to share the following with you:

America loves immigrants; this is who we are as a nation: a haven of opportunity and liberty to those escaping tyranny. And everyone who immigrates to America has a gift, a talent, an idea that they can contribute to building America or making America great. But those who immigrate must do it legally for three reasons: Immigration gives you human dignity and ample opportunity, enables you to work for higher wages, and keeps you and America safe. Those who come to us from Mexico and South America are escaping communist regimes, ruthless dictators, economic hardship, and murderous drug cartels. Those who are refugees from Syria and other Arab nations are fleeing horrific political conditions in which life has no value and destiny has no hope. Indeed, you don't want any of the above following you to America! That's why you're left!

Under the administration of President Trump, the Deferred Action for Childhood Arrivals (DACA), initiated by the Obama administration, came under scrutiny. Trump's January 2018 Immigration "Framework" proposal included replacing DACA with a "path of citizenship" for DACA recipients and allocating $25 billion for expanded border infrastructure consistent with Trump's Executive Order 13767. This order, however, was revoked by Trump's successor, Joe Biden.

Such reforms existed to ensure legalization and endless opportunity under the banner of the Free while imposing necessary legislation to deter drug cartels, communist insurgents, terrorists, and terrorist networks from finding refuge or opportunity in the United States of America![72]

"The American flag is the most recognized symbol of freedom and democracy in the world."

Virginia Foxx

CHAPTER THREE

The House of Lies

"for we have made lies our refuge, and under falsehood have we hid ourselves." Isaiah 28:17

೮೦

Immigration is not the only web that was spun and cockatrice egg that was hatched, but it is an important one.

Before we move into other issues that challenged the integrity of Washington D.C. and Trump's Presidency, let's look at Washington's house of lies.

Every President has their secrets, and not a few have been caught in a lie or two. Take Nixon and his Watergate scandal, which is probably no less scandalous than Hillary and her emails or, most recently, John Podesta and his emails. Nobody likes lying, but there is a difference between telling a lie or relaying faulty intelligence and being a pathological liar.

Remember the saying, "birds of a feather flock together?" Pathological liars beget other pathological liars. And before you know it, they have collectively built their entire house on lies.

After taking office in January 2009, President Obama was caught in 1,249 documented cases of lying, lawbreaking, corruption, cronyism, hypocrisy, and waste, according to Tim Brown from Freedom Outpost[73] and Daniel Alman, blogger of Dan on Squirrel Hill.[74] That is more than any other or even all Presidents combined.

With this record, no one can say with an honest heart or straight face that our former President didn't have a pathological lying problem. And if we consider that like begets like, Hillary probably clocks in at a close second.

∞

Pathological Liars

What is a pathological liar, and how do you spot them?[75] According to Tamara Hill, MS, LPC, whose article was featured in PsychCentral, there are two types of pathological liars, the "compulsive" liar and the "skillful" liar:

> There are Pathological liars who quite frankly cannot help telling so many lies. . ..Their world is much different from ours. But some liars are gratified by telling lies, are good at it, and do not regret anything they have ever said. These individuals are "skillful" liars who attempt to evade and

harm everyone they come across in their lives. In fact, these liars would meet the diagnostic criteria for antisocial personality disorder (or sociopathy). They also tell truths in ways that give incorrect perspectives. In other words, they misleadingly tell the truth to cause people to view things incorrectly. Such individuals enjoy and get much gratification from keeping you confused and believing their stories. The experience of watching a "victim" run through the maze of confusion gives gratification to most liars.[76]

When I read the above definition, my mind flashed to an incident in our nation's consciousness, the death of Alton Sterling. A young 37-year-old black man who was eulogized as a loving father of five by the Black Lives Matter movement and whose death was used to incite riots in Louisiana and throughout the country.

Mignon Chambers, Sterling's sister, told WAFB-TV that he was a father of five who had been selling CDs outside the store for years. "I really wanna know more about what happened, about the whole situation, because my brother didn't deserve it. He didn't deserve it at all," Chambers told the news station. Sharida Sterling, his cousin, told The Advocate, "He would have never fought the police, he wouldn't have pulled a gun, he would have been too scared." (Facebook)

Truthfully, no one deserves to die unjustly. And God knows there have been justifiable injustices committed toward the African-American community. But that does not give license to commit falsehood. What Alton's sister and cousin told WAFB-TV was an untruth. A misrepresentation that could be construed as intentionally misleading the public. The truth is that Alton had a police record of assaulting cops and a rap sheet that included rape, gang banging, substance abuse, illegal firearms, failure to pay child support, domestic abuse, and the list goes on. To paint this young man as a harmless soul to the public was wrong. My mother always taught me, "if you play with fire, sooner or later, you will get burned." And unfortunately, Alton's second chances had expired. This was not a white cop who hated the black boy crime scene. This appears to be a young man who had pushed his luck once too many times.[77][78] Michael Brown, too was a young man who had just robbed a convenience store and almost took out a cop's eye. The cop, Darren Wilson, was accused of assassinating Michael Brown's character by stating the events leading up to the incident—i.e., he robbed a convenience store.

What did President Obama have to say about Alton Sterling? Very little, but what he did do was perpetuate a falsehood.

&

PsychCentral

Tamara Hill, MS. LPC, writes that six telling signs enable you to recognize when someone is a pathological liar:[79]

1. **Know that a pathological liar will study you**: The liar's goal may be hidden, but you can count on the fact that they don't want you to know the truth. In order to evade

someone, you certainly need to study the person and examine what that person might or might not believe. Liars, often sociopaths, are known to "study" the person they hope to take advantage of. In other words, they look for weaknesses.

2. **Don't forget that the liar lacks empathy:** As hard as it is to believe, it is true. The liar has no moral consciousness of how their lying behavior may make you feel.

3. **Normal people feel guilty and are relieved when you change the topic or stop asking questions:** A pathological liar is not fazed. You will rarely if ever, see emotion.

4. **All liars do not do the common things you think liars do:** Believe it or not, liars do not always touch their noses, shift in their seats or from one foot to the next, or even look sneaky when lying. Some sociopaths have learned to evade people with direct eye contact, sociable smiles, and humor. Trust your instincts and discernment. What do their eyes tell you? What does their behavior or laughter tell you?

5. **The most sneaky liars are manipulative:** I once heard someone say, "we all manipulate." While this might be true to a certain degree, the liar tends to manipulate more than anyone else and has learned how to become a "pro" at doing it. There is nothing impressive about the dangerous or evil manipulator.

6. **Pathological liars exhibit strange behaviors:** Some research suggests that pathological liars show no discomfort when caught lying, while others indicate that

liars may become aggressive and angry. The bottom line is that no pathological liar is the same.

ॐ

1, 249 Lies

If you were to google "Obama's Lies," you would be shocked at the number of articles and lists. From PolitiFact to the Pentagon, voices protested the lying that came forth from Obama and his administration as much as they protested the crass rhetoric from President Trump's mouth. However, there remains a difference.

As mentioned above, Dan from Squirrel Hill[80] documented 1,249 well-researched lies dated from August 15, 2013, to July 22, 2016. Let's look at a few of these lies.

Lie #1: President Obama had an administration full of lobbyists after promising he wouldn't have any:

On November 15, 2007, in Las Vegas, Nevada, Obama said that lobbyists " . . . will not work in my White House." However, by February 2010, he had more than 40 lobbyists working in his administration. According to Timothy Carney of the Washington Examiner, Obama had "hired more than 40 ex-lobbyists now populate top jobs in the Obama administration, including three Cabinet secretaries, the Director of Central Intelligence, and many senior White House officials."[8182]

Of those 40 ex-lobbyists, 10% (4) were given elite staff positions in the White House and State Department by the Center for American Progress (CAP). This liberal think tank has a sister organization Center for American Progress Action Fund (CAP Action). CAP's directors and funders include none other than George Soros.[83] Here is the 2009 message from CAP:[84]

> The Center for American Progress—which has emerged as perhaps Washington's most influential idea factory in the age of Obama—is launching a major new war room, to be staffed by nearly a dozen people, that will focus on driving the White House's message and agenda, I'm told. . ..The new war room—Progressive Media—represents a serious ratcheting up of efforts to present a united liberal front in the coming policy wars. The goal of the war room will be to do hard-hitting research that boils down complex policy questions into usable talking points and narratives that play well in the media and build public support for the White House's policy goals. . ..The war room—a joint project of CAP Action Fund and Media Matters Action Network — will be headed by well-known liberal operative Tara McGuinness who worked on John Kerry's presidential campaign and, during the Bush years, was a major player in the anti-war movement.

Lie #2: President Obama had close ties to Wall St. but pretended to support Occupy Wall Street:

Although Obama claimed to support the Occupy Wall St. movement, the truth is that in 2011, he raised more money from Wall St. than any other candidate during the previous 20 years. In early 2012, Obama held a fundraiser where Wall St. investment bankers and hedge fund managers paid $35,800 to attend. In October 2011, Obama hired Broderick Johnson, a longtime Wall Street lobbyist, as his new senior campaign adviser. Johnson had worked as a lobbyist for JP Morgan Chase, Bank of America, Fannie Mae, Comcast, Microsoft, and the oil industry.[85]

Lie #3: President Obama gave tax dollars to AIG executives, then pretended to be outraged about it:

Obama signed a "stimulus" bill that spent money on bonuses for AIG executives. Before signing this bill, Obama said, "when I'm president, I will go line by line to make sure that we are not spending money unwisely." However, after reading "line by line" and signing the "stimulus" bill that protected the AIG bonuses, Obama pretended to be shocked and outraged at the bonuses and said, "Under these circumstances, it's hard to understand how derivative traders at AIG warranted any bonuses at all, much less $165 million in extra pay . .. How do they justify this outrage to the taxpayers who are keeping the company afloat?" He also said that he would "pursue every single legal avenue to block these bonuses."

Lie #4: President Obama ordered a private company to fire 1,000 employees:

In 2011, after Boeing had hired 1,000 new employees to work at its new factory in South Carolina, the Obama administration ordered Boeing to shut down the factory because it was non-union.

Lie #5: President Obama lied about putting health care negotiations on C-SPAN:

Although Obama had made a campaign promise to have all the health care reform negotiations broadcast on C-SPAN, he broke that promise after being elected. The secrecy of these negotiations was so vital that U.S. Congresswoman and Speaker of the House Nancy Pelosi (D-California) said, "We have to pass the bill so that you can find out what is in it."

Other lies listed on the site include: (173) Hired a retarded man to sell illegal drugs and guns and then arrested him for doing so; (174) Secretly obtained phone records from Associated Press reporters and editors; (178) Falsely accused a law-abiding news reporter (James Rosen) of being "an aider and abettor and co-conspirator" in a criminal investigation; (500) Illegally tried to avoid disclosure of a foreign aid directive that he had signed.[8687]

I have posted links to Dan's website in the endnotes. It lists the many facets of lies, corruption, and deception that have built Washington's house of lies. Honestly, it was overwhelming to go through the process of reading them—it just brought tears to my eyes to see so much injustice coming from and around our former Commander-in-Chief.

The problem with lying is that it weaves a web of deception over those under it—you might say it casts a spell or brings a curse. Of late, when I listen to sects of Washington's perpetuation of these same lies, it reaffirms how entangled in the Washington Web all associated with the Obama and Biden administrations are—knowingly or unknowingly, for good or bad reasons.

℃

Does Trump Lie?

After reading the above, you're probably asking yourself, "what about Trump?" Especially after watching all the news surrounding the classified files from Mar-a-Lago and, most recently, the alleged fraud accusations.

So, let's ask the question, "Does Trump lie?" The answer is most likely, "yes." Most leaders tell a lie here and there, especially under duress. Have you ever lied when put on the spot?

There were statements made throughout his campaign that, when fact-checked, were considered false statements or possible lies. With that said, "what would make his lying different from former President Obama, Hillary Clinton, or Joe Biden?

I would like to suggest context and intent. Given Trump's track record of opposing Washington's corruption and lies, it is improbable that he would intentionally lie to mislead the American people. Neither are there any signs that Trump is a pathological liar. On the contrary, most people find him too blunt and honest about America's problems. And when faced with his follies, he fesses up. He doesn't weave another lie.

While attending the University of Haifa, Israel, I was asked about Trump by a studious and bright young man from China. He felt very attacked by Trump's accusations about China's currency manipulation and trade ethics. I told him that in no way was Trump attacking the Chinese people but the ethics of the Government. He then stated what many of us have said, "I just wish he didn't have to be so forthright about it!" There you have it—that's the comparison we have when confronting Washington's house of lies.

"When leaders choose to make themselves bidders at an auction of popularity, their talents, in the construction of the state, will be of no service. They will become flatterers instead of legislators; the instruments, not the guides, of the people."

Edmund Burke

CHAPTER FOUR

American Democracy

"By humility and the fear of the LORD are riches, honor, and life." Proverbs 22:4

൪

Have you ever thought that maybe, just maybe, the 2016 and 2020 elections were not between Hillary Clinton or Joe Biden and Donald Trump?

You might be thinking, "of course, the election was between Hillary/Biden and Trump"—really? Yes, in the eyes of the American public, the election appeared to be between these candidates, but behind the scenes, we may find an entirely different story. And if so, what story? What could the 2016 and 2020 national elections have been about other than the election of a new President?

First, I would like to suggest that the 2016 election was about the future direction of our nation, and the 2020 election was about stopping Trump. This chapter and the remainder of this book will focus on the 2016 election. A sequel will follow that connects the dots of the 2020 election.

Let's begin with the appearance of the Obama administration. For many, Obama was the man leading America in a more progressive liberal direction. However, as we learned in the first few chapters, others shaped America's progressive trend in the shadows. Obama was the voice and vehicle of a movement that transcended the democratic party, a network of leaders and organizations influenced by George Soros and the Open Society Foundation—the man who funded Hillary Clinton's 2016 campaign.

This understanding, therefore, begs the question, could the 2016 election have been about two men with two different world views—one man who upholds the Constitution and the foundational principles that made America great, and another man who abhors the Constitution and desperately wants it replaced with the U.N.'s Universal Declaration of Human Rights to create a new world order? An order of the borderless, "Open Society?"

From an American perspective, questioning whether the U.S. is an "open society" or not is preposterous. America is a bastion of hope to the masses, and a republic that offers its citizens and its immigrant's endless opportunity, liberty, and hope. No country provides its citizens with what America does. In America, even the poorest of the poor can find assistance and, if desired, run down to the local Starbucks for a morning coffee.

The American culture is the most heterogeneous and opportunity-driven in the world. Americans love to give, love to help, and love to live life to its fullest. Not to mention, America comprises every nation, tribe, and tongue.

And we love to lead. We have been a role model of freedom, liberty, and justice throughout the world, that is—until the Obama administration. Yet, even today, if I ask an Israeli, "would you like to live in America?" The answer is a passionate, "yes; I would love to live in America." And that holds with almost every foreigner I meet when I am overseas. For example, one day, while discussing visas during a national security class, a beautiful young lady from Serbia yelled out, "I would love a visa to America."

This portrayal of America as a beacon of light for the world needs to be understood in light of the forces trying to extinguish its light. What follows is a scenario that reveals the depth to which citizens worldwide desire to come to America.

During an eye-opening lecture about the emotions of Egyptian youth during the Arab Spring, I saw firsthand how they used graffiti to express their feelings toward government and society. Many young artists painted murals on walls depicting the deep despair, anger, and frustration dominating Egyptian society during the Arab Spring uprising.

What I did not expect was the question Egyptian youth were asking themselves. During the deepest, darkest night of their nation's struggle for freedom—the younger generation asked only one question, "where are you, America? You are the one we look to for freedom — where are you?" This was the question that plagued their precious hearts and minds. They could not understand how a nation that represented freedom, fueled and ignited their desire for change and democracy, and then called for the removal of their dictator could leave them to fight alone, to die alone—all in the name of 'American freedom.'

"Where are you, America, when we need you? You are the one we look to for freedom — where are you?"

The Arab youth didn't ask, where are you Europe, where are you China, where are you Russia, where are you United Nations, where are you NATO? They asked, "where are you, America?"

As I stared at these murals and heard their cries, my eyes filled with tears, and my heart wept. I asked myself, "where were we?" And answered me, "we were too busy trying not to be America."

I invite you to ask yourself, "where are you, America?" Are you the America I grew up in? Are you still the America that champions righteousness and hope to the world? Are you still an America of opportunity? Will you be there for me, my family, and my neighbor when we need you? Or are you too busy trying to be something you're not?"

଼

America's Honor

Sadly, even though Americans may see America as an "open society," that is not how George Soros, former President Obama, Hillary Clinton, or European global leaders see America. They see a "closed society"—a society that believes in an old Asiatic tyrant called 'God' and a national declaration that supports that belief: "We hold these truths to be self-evident, that all men are created equal, that they are endowed by their Creator with certain unalienable Rights, that among these are Life, Liberty and the Pursuit of Happiness."

Furthermore, they see the American Constitution as an obstacle to the "open society." Why? Because it has checks and balances to ensure that America never falls into the tyrannical trap of a dictatorship. And, in a more elusive way, they see our Constitution and governmental order as outdated as God Himself. Why? Because although the idea of democracy can be traced back to the enlightenment period of history, the American Constitution is unique and unlike any other constitution in the world. Our Constitution is based on a distinct biblical pattern of government.[88]

American citizens must understand that the United States of America came out of the British commonwealth, a monarchy. A monarchy ruled by a king who represented God in the eyes of the people. It is also crucial to understand that the democratic Western world, referred to as Europe today, was monarchal until the late 1800s and early 1900s. On the other hand, America was settled by men and women escaping monarchal tyranny. Religious freedom was the most sought-after liberty from the 1500s forward, and the Bible inspired our break from England.

The shift in Europe from monarchal to democratic changed more than political powers. For example, when France got rid of its last king during the French Revolution—it also got rid of God. The people considered the kings in Europe and the Commonwealth as God's representatives. Hence, *No king is equated to No God*—the people rule. To the people, God was the king's God, and the king was a hypocritical tyrant. Therefore, God was viewed as a hypocritical tyrant too.

However, that was not the case with our founding fathers. They believed that the God of Abraham, Isaac, and Jacob was a God of the people—one who watched over them to do them good, not evil. And because this was their perspective, two things happened in the forming of the United States of America.

Firstly, as a people, we entered into a covenant with God. What nation, apart from Israel, has ever entered into a covenant with God? And what does that mean exactly?

Carole Keller, a prolific writer on American restoration, writes,

So, you see, between Europe and the United States, there are two distinct democracies. The United States governing philosophy is based upon the ancient framework of the Ten Commandments. Europe also follows a democratic form of government but is not established upon covenantal relations. When comparing America to ancient Israel, the difference is that Israel was a theocracy, and America developed as a Republic without conscription to a national religion. Thus, America would advance the greatest personal freedom for all people, ultimately giving America a decisive edge in maintaining peace and order. The promise is unto us, as it was upon Israel, that, if we keep covenant with God, no enemy nation would be able to stand before us. "Every place whereupon the soles of your feet shall tread shall be yours…No man shall be able to stand before you: for the LORD your God shall lay the fear of you and the dread of you upon all the land that ye shall tread upon, as he hath said unto you."[89]

A covenant is a two-way agreement that is very hard to break. In fact, the covenant between God and Israel cannot be broken. Of this agreement, the prophet Jeremiah wrote,

Thus saith the LORD, which gives the sun for a light by day, and the ordinances of thereon and of the stars for a light by night, which divides the sea when the waves thereof roar; the LORD of hosts is his name: If those ordinances depart from before me, said the LORD, then the seed of Israel also shall cease from being a nation before me forever.[90]

Secondly, America's government is established by the people and for the people. And, in the case of tyranny, the people have the right to abolish the government and restore it to its covenantal foundations. Our foundations began with the Declaration of Independence and were subsequently established by George Washington and the Constitution of the United States of America.

The Declaration of Independence is quite a moving document filled with nuances of revelation. Yet, it distinctly puts the Creator as the chief governing agent of America. And to this ideal, the people humbly yoke themselves, as is exemplified in the final words of The Declaration of Independence:[91]

> We, therefore, the Representatives of the United States of America, in General Congress, Assembled, appealing to the Supreme Judge of the world for the rectitude of our intentions, do, in the Name, and by Authority of the good People of these Colonies, solemnly publish and declare, That these United Colonies are, and of Right ought to be Free and Independent States; that they are Absolved from all Allegiance to the British Crown, and that all political connection between them and the State of Great Britain, is and ought to be totally dissolved; and that as Free and Independent States, they have full Power to levy War, conclude Peace, contract Alliances, establish Commerce, and to do all other Acts and Things which Independent States may of right do. And for the support of this Declaration, with a firm reliance on the protection of divine Providence, we mutually pledge to each other our Lives, our Fortunes, and our sacred Honor.

With the signed Declaration and an unratified Constitution, George Washington was nominated as the first President of the United States of America thirteen years later.

He gave the first Presidential oath and the first inaugural address on April 30, 1789. This was when heaven and the United States of America formed an invincible bond. George Washington placed his hand on the bible and opened to Genesis chapter 49. He said, "I do solemnly swear that I will faithfully execute the Office of the President of the United States, and will to the best of my ability, preserve, protect and defend the Constitution of the United States. So help me, God."[92]

Afterward, he walked into the Senate Chamber and delivered his first inaugural address, opening with a prayer:

It would be peculiarly improper to omit in this first official Act my fervent supplications to that Almighty Being who rules over the Universe, who presides in the Councils of Nations, and whose providential aids can supply every human defect, that his benediction may consecrate to the liberties and happiness of the People of the United States, a Government instituted by themselves for these essential purposes.

Washington continues,

No People can be bound to acknowledge and adore the invisible hand, which conducts the Affairs of men more than the People of the United States. Every step by which they have advanced to the character of an independent nation seems to have been distinguished by some token of providential agency. . ..Since we ought to be no less persuaded that the propitious smiles of Heaven can never be expected on a nation that disregards the eternal rules of order and right, which Heaven itself has ordained: And since the preservation of the sacred fire of liberty, and the destiny of the republican model of Government, are justly considered as deeply, perhaps as finally staked, on the experiment entrusted to the hands of the American people."

ဆ

A Republican Model

We understand that the forming of America brought forth the tenets of a Republican model of Government. The anchor of this model was the belief that the Almighty's hand was upon America and His providence would ensure that all her needs were met and that, over time, freedoms would be established, prejudices would be abolished, and justice rewarded to the citizens of this great country. And upon these two beliefs, imbued within the pages of the Torah, was the Constitution and its Bill of rights[93] written and subsequently ratified on December 15, 1791.

Have you ever read the Constitution? It's an amazing document replete with the guiding principles people need to build a just, righteous, and wise nation.

Of it, Matthew Spalding wrote,

Consider the Constitution. The separation of powers and the system of checks and balances thwart governmental despotism and promote responsibility in public representatives. The legitimate constitutional amendment process allows democratic reform while elevating the document above the popular passions of the moment, thereby encouraging deliberation and patience in the people. The law inspires caution and encourages mutual checks in our representatives, thereby confining them to their constitutional responsibilities and preventing a spirit of encroachment by the government. The people learn from the law-making process to curb their passions for immediate political change and abide by the legitimate legal process. The demands of sound public policy cause the people to be moderate and circumspect. Good opinions of the people, and good government, have a complementary effect on politics.[94]

Yes, "We the people of the United States, in order to form a more perfect Union, establish Justice, insure domestic Tranquility, provide for the common Defense, promote the general Welfare, and secure the Blessings of Liberty to ourselves and our Posterity, do ordain and establish this Constitution for the United States of America."

With that said, a Constitution alone cannot govern the hearts of mankind. For that, there needs to be self-government which George Washington, Thomas Jefferson, James Madison, and Benjamin Frankly all elaborated upon.

James Madison wrote:

[T]he citizens of the United States are responsible for the greatest trust ever confided to a political society. If justice, good faith, honor, gratitude, and all the other qualities which ennoble the character of a nation and fulfill the ends of government be the fruits of our establishments, the cause of liberty will acquire dignity and luster, which it has never yet enjoyed, and an example will be set, which cannot but have the most favorable influence on the rights of Mankind. If on the other side, our government should be unfortunately blotted with the reverse of these cardinal virtues, the great cause which we have engaged to vindicate will be dishonored and betrayed; the last and fairest experiment in favor of the rights of human nature will be turned against them, and their patrons and friends exposed to be insulted and silenced by the votaries of tyranny and usurpation.

George Washington continued this exhortation in his Farewell Address:

"Religion and morality are indispensable supports." Religion and morality aid good government by teaching men their moral obligations and creating the conditions for decent political life. Thomas Jefferson, the great defender of rights and liberty, put it bluntly when he said that the American people "are inherently independent of all but the moral law."[95]

So, the critical components of America's Democracy are a Republican government and a moral law model.

*The Obama administration has consistently refused to
recognize Jerusalem as Israeli territory,
let alone as the capital of Israel.*

Ben Shapiro

&

CHAPTER FIVE

European Democracy

*"If the foundations be destroyed, what can the righteous
do?" Psalm 11:3*

ℰℴ

Our Republican model of government was not without
its two opposing parties. At the time of the
Constitution's conception, there were the Federalists
and the Anti-Federalists. Anti-Federalists were those who were
in opposition to a robust federal government and the
ratification of the Constitution drafted in 1787. It was not until
the Bill of Rights was added to the Constitution that the Anti-
Federalists would ratify it. Their preference was for power to
remain with states and local governments. On the other hand,
the Federalists supported a strong national government and the
ratification of the Constitution. They believed the government
needed to play a formidable role in managing the debt and
tensions following the American Revolution.[96]

The first Federalist party formed by Alexander Hamilton operated from 1792 to 1824. Other famous

Federalists were George Washington and John Adams. Anti-Federalists included Thomas Jefferson, James Monroe, Patrick Henry, and Samuel Adams.

Here we get a glimpse into the contention between the two parties over the ratification of the Bill of Rights:[97]

One of the many points of contention between Federalists and Anti-Federalists was the Constitution's lack of a bill of rights that would place specific limits on government power. Federalists argued that the Constitution did not need a Bill of Rights because the people and the states kept any powers not given to the federal government. Anti-Federalists held that a bill of rights was necessary to safeguard individual liberty.

Regardless of the bantering back and forth over the need for government safeguards, there were no qualms about God and the use of His human rights laws as the moral underpinning necessary to sustain this new, and ultimately great, Republic we know as, The United States of America.

This leads us seamlessly into the next series of historical developments that play a role in developing Europe's democracy. And who leads the way? None other than Thomas Jefferson, the Anti-Federalist.

கை

The Right of Man and of the Citizen

In August 1789, under the leadership of Napoleon, the National Constituent Assembly adopted the *Declaration of the Right of Man and of the Citizen.* The significance of its content and origin cannot be underestimated; not only did it become the foundational document of the French Revolution and the basis for the United Nations Universal Declaration of Human Rights adopted in 1948, but it also had a direct impact on liberty and democracy throughout all of Europe and the world.[98]

Its origins, though, in principle, are biblical and distinctly American. Inspired by the American Revolution and the Enlightenment principles of human rights, General Lafayette worked closely with Thomas Jefferson, the principal architect of the Declaration of Independence. It is not a coincidence that Thomas Jefferson was in France as a U.S. diplomat when this bill was constructed. Jefferson could draw from numerous foundational documents that formed the ideal of America, including The Virginia Declaration of Rights and The U.S. Bill of Rights.[99] His influence is clearly seen in the first line of the French Declaration: "Article I - Men are born and remain free and equal in rights. Social distinctions can be founded only on the common good."

The Declaration also ushered in the end of feudalism by asserting popular sovereignty over the divine right of kings— a principle expressed by Benjamin Franklin, "In free governments, the rulers are the servants and the people their superiors and sovereigns."[100] Thus favored treatment of nobility and clergy was eliminated as stated, "All the citizens, being equal in the eyes of the law, are equally admissible to all public dignities, places, and employments, according to their capacity and without distinction other than that of their virtues and their talents."[101] It was the beginning of the end of the Holy Roman Empire and monarchal Europe as they knew it.

What is absent in the *Declaration of the Right of Man and of the Citizen* and its subsequent offspring, the *United Nations Universal Declaration of Human Rights* is the mention of God—the true source of human rights. This is, of course, the telltale sign of France and, ultimately, Europe's rejection of God and its removal of kings. The other aspect absent in France's declaration is "moral law."

From the French Revolution until World War II, there were numerous changes to the landscape of monarchial Europe. One such change took place in Germany with the establishment of the Weimar Republic—Germany's first democratic form of Government. Sadly, it was short-lived due to the rise of Christian Nationalism and the ideology of the State. The "ideology of the state" is crucial to understanding "where God went" when he was removed alongside monarchal rule.

It was Georg Hegel,[102] a renowned Protestant theologian, and German philosopher, who, in his assessment of power and ownership of the rights of man, transferred all from the religious institutions to the State:

The Universal is to be found in the State. . ..The State is the Divine Idea as it exists on earth. . ..We must, therefore, worship the State as the manifestation of the Divine on earth. . ..The State is the march of God through the world.[103]

Karl Popper noted that Hegel's view was "absolute moral authority of the State, which overrules all personal morality, all conscience."[104] And as the bearer of the Ten Commandments and its enigma Christianity Martin Bormann, head of the Parteikanzlei (Nazi Party Chancellery) and Hitler's private secretary, publicly stated:

National Socialist and Christian concepts are incompatible. . ..Our National Socialist worldview stands on a much higher level than the concepts of Christianity, which in their essentials were taken over from Judaism. For this reason, too, we can do without Christianity.[105]

So, let's recap the last few statements. First, we see that moral authority has shifted from God and self-government to the State as a Divine Idea to be worshiped. Just as the king was looked upon as the one who ruled in God's stead, now the State is seen as the authority that rules in God's stead. The scary part is what follows.

Hegel, Popper, and Bormann saw the state as "man's moral conscience." There was no need for self-government or individual thought; the State did it for you! It became your conscience!

Let's consider the effects of this ideological shift in Germany. It meant that the State had the power to develop your values and moral compass, apart from God. This led to the State no longer needing Christianity or Judaism for guidance because the National Socialist worldview reached a much higher plane.

And if you think that's frightening, hold onto your jaw because it's about to drop.

૭૦

God is Dead

Nothing underscores these developments in Europe more than Fredrick Nietzsche and his famous observation: God is dead, and the church killed him. Now, if society wants to get rid of God, how would they do it?

Consider that, even though the king was removed, the moral code of the Ten Commandments was still rooted in the Catholic and Protestant citizens of Christian Europe. So, the next logical step was to remove it. And that was precisely what the Nazi party and Hitler set out to do.

Of the Ten Commandments, Hitler said,

The day will come when I shall hold up against these commandments the tables of a new law. And history will recognize our movement as the great battle for humanity's liberation, a liberation from the curse of Mount Sinai, from the dark stammering of nomads who could no more trust their own sound instincts, who could understand the divine only in the form of a tyrant who orders one to do the very things one doesn't like. This is what we are fighting against: the masochistic spirit of self-torment, the curse of so-called morals, idolized to protect the weak from the strong in the face of the immortal law of battle, the great law of divine nature. Against these so-called Ten Commandments against them, we are fighting.[106]

Yes, you read it correctly. Hitler blamed the ills of the world on the Ten Commandments or, as he said, "the curse of so-called morals."

So, let's look at these morals and ask ourselves, "what exactly are the Ten Commandments if not the bedrock of true human rights?"

To the founding fathers of America, the Ten Commandments are the foundation of what men call the "issues of life." They are the plumb line of right and wrong, good and evil, holy and profane within the conscience of mankind. They are the divine moral code that Herbert Huffmon, an expert in Old Testament studies, says "concern matters of fundamental importance in both Judaism and Christianity." He writes,

They reveal the greatest obligation of mankind—to worship only God. They underscore the value of human life and the greatest injury to a person—murder. They highlight the covenant of marriage and reveal the greatest injury to family bonds—adultery. They teach men ethics in business while emphasizing that the greatest injury to commerce and law is fraud and lying—bearing false witness. They instruct children on the greatest inter-generational obligation—honor to parents. They show us that the greatest obligation to a community is truthfulness and that theft is the greatest injury to your neighbor and his moveable property.[107]

In the Christian New Testament, five of the Ten Commandments are mentioned with their association with neighborly love:

Owe no man anything, but to love one another: for he that loves another has fulfilled the law. For this, you shall not commit adultery, you shall not kill, you shall not steal, you shall not bear false witness, you shall not covet; and if there be any other commandments, it is briefly comprehended in this saying, namely, you shall love thy neighbor as thyself. Love works no ill to his neighbor: therefore, love is the fulfillment of the law.[108]

Sadly, the very Commandments that bring life, liberty, and the pursuit of happiness to Israel, the United States, and any country that adopts them, have become the yoke that every generation struggles with and that every government attempts to unburden themselves from.

We learn from Hermann Rauschning,[109] well known for his book *Voice of Destruction* and other eyewitness accounts of Hitler's ranting, that "Hitler and his malleable henchmen hated God's law. They knew that it was the only thing that stood between them and their new world order. And that the God of the Bible as described by Hitler was "that Asiatic tyrant." Also, real freedom was freedom from God's law."[110] I might add that by hating God's laws; they innately hated the Jews—for they were and are the bearers of God's covenants and His laws.

This brings us to the two points of separation between the European and American democracy: God and His Moral Law.

&

Church and State

Now you may be reading this and wholeheartedly believe in the separation of Church and State. And you should. The last thing you want is the Church running the State or the Federal government. Can you imagine that? Scary, right? Just figuring out which Church would rule would require how many committees. No thanks!

On the other hand, a strong, stable government is rooted in a foundational faith.

For example, China is a communist country that boasts three religions: Confucianism, Taoism, and Buddhism. The official position of the Chinese Communist Party-State government is Marxist-Leninist-Maoist atheism which believes that religion will die out as social conditions evolve. Even though this is the official position of the government and its members must support such, the reality is that the government is funding a revival of Confucianism, and over

20% of its society practices Buddhism. The Chinese government's motive for supporting Confucianism is to counter the Western influence and replace it with anti-Western and anti-modern nationalism. Also, on the fringe, the government allows for forms of state-controlled Protestantism and Chinese Catholicism.

That said, an anti-Western agenda does not mean anti-moral or anti-value sentiment. On the contrary, Asian culture holds the family unit and its social values central to society. Hence, they see Western civilization as morally bankrupt—anything goes in the name of tolerance under the banner of Human Rights. This is a threat to their societal core. Amidst all its religious diversity, from atheism to Buddhism, Confucianism to state-controlled Christian institutions, a moral framework is woven into its religious base. Also, there is an emerging ethos of biblical ethics. This is likely due to the shifting religious landscape of China towards a Judeo-Christianity. This is confirmed by a burgeoning underground Christian movement estimated at around 35 million[111] and a growing Israeli-Jewish presence in cities like Shanghai.[112]

How ironic would it be if China became a Judeo-Christian nation while America wasted away into nihilism? Not possible? It's already happening. One of the most significant movements in China, the "Back to Jerusalem" movement, is a Christian-based organization that believes China plays a huge role in restoring Israel and returning the Messiah.

India is another rising superstar. Its national religion may be Hinduism, reflected in its cultural practice, but its

Constitution is structured after the U.S. Constitution. And although much of India's leadership is part of the elite ruling caste system, its moral underpinnings closely relate to the Torah.[113] Once again, we see a shift towards accepting a Judeo-Christian belief system. India is also a close friend and ally of Israel.

Russia and African countries like the Congo, Uganda, and Nigeria are good examples of governments that have incorporated a semblance of a biblical moral framework into the foundational underpinnings of their society. By no means is the Russian government even remotely accepting of biblical faith, apart from its national pseudo-religion encapsulated in the Russian Orthodox Church. But, as a Marxist communist government, it has repeatedly shunned President Obama's push towards a more liberal human rights platform that abandon's God's gender laws. Nigeria, too, objected to Obama's call for a more progressive human rights platform; it directly conflicted with Nigeria's collective conscience and moral law. Nigeria considers itself a Christian nation currently in a life and death battle against radical Islam—another faith system that upholds an appearance of God's law often without components of grace and mercy.

So, to recap, we are seeing countries that hold dear their foundational moral and cultural ethics emerging on the global stage. While Western civilization is throwing off all moral constraints in the name of "Human Rights."

And what about America?

As we continue to desensitize our moral conscience and ignore our founding fathers' foundational tenets, we spiral further into civil and political anarchy.

Consider that America is now embroiled in violent racial debates, unprecedented murders of citizens and law enforcement, and indoctrination of youth that fosters a non-gender godless society with a throw your conscience out the door political revolution that has created a cesspool of iniquity in government. The gaping hole of moral and spiritual decline within American society is filled with drug cartels, terrorist cells, illegal immigration, anti-American and anti-God ideologies, increasing rates of suicide, staggering national debt, and a lascivious society that has very little self-control. Wow, that's a mouthful—is it that bad? I hope not.

On that note, I think it is time to reconsider not the role of the Church in governmental affairs but the role of God's laws that uphold human rights and the biblical precepts that undergirded our government and made America great in the first place. These are the Laws that George Washington, Thomas Jefferson, and James Madison spoke of and adopted. These principles enabled our nation to emerge from European tyranny and rise to lead the Free World. God's laws and instruction are the answer to the social justice America, and the nations are desperately crying for.

ℴ

Post-WWII: 1968

Immediately following WWII, the nations gathered to adopt a solution to the atrocities of the war. What was their answer? *The United Nations Universal Declaration of Human Rights.* For the most part, this declaration remained in limbo throughout the Cold War, except in the year 1968.[114]

1968 was a year of unprecedented civil unrest in America and worldwide. It was the end of America's role in the Vietnam War.

Let's deviate for a second to ensure our readers understand the Vietnam War and America's role in this war. The following assertion, taken from HistoryNet, provides an excellent summary:[115]

The Vietnam War is commonly used for the Second Indochina War, 1954–1973. It refers to the period when the United States and other members of the SEATO (Southeast Asia Treaty Organization) joined the forces of the Republic of South Vietnam to contest the communist Viet Cong (VC) and the North Vietnamese Army (NVA). The U.S. had the largest foreign military presence and directed the war from 1965 to 1968. For this reason, it is known as the American War in Vietnam today. The war was a direct result of the First Indochina War (1946–1954) between France, which claimed Vietnam as a colony, and the communist forces, then known as Viet Minh. In 1973, a "third" Vietnam war was a continuation between North and South Vietnam, but without significant U.S.

involvement. It ended with a communist victory in April 1975.

The Vietnam War was the longest in U.S. history until the war in Afghanistan began in 2002 and continues at this writing (2013). It was incredibly divisive in the U.S., Europe, Australia, and elsewhere. Because the U.S. failed to achieve a military victory, the Republic of South Vietnam was ultimately taken over by North Vietnam; the Vietnam experience became known as "the only war America ever lost." It remains a controversial topic affecting political and military decisions today.

The Vietnam War and, more specifically, the TET offensive[116] awakened the American public to the reality of war.[117] Before the Vietnam war, Americans had never been exposed to the blood, guts, and horrors of war in "real-time." Radio and movie theaters updated the nation on the details of previous wars to ensure the American public was not exposed to the gorier side of war. Even when the unimaginable horrors of the death camps and the slaughter of six million Jews were revealed, Americans were deeply disturbed and horrified. Still, even then, it was not in "real-time."

However, the Vietnam War and the TET offensive were televised in "real-time." When the American people saw the shooting of innocent Vietnamese and the burning of their homes, they could no longer condone such a War. The "real-time" exposure violated the American collective conscience causing the younger generations to take the streets. Protests and civil unrest turned the war into a political nightmare manifesting the abandonment of military honor and respect. Such reproach upon U.S. soldiers was undeserving. However, the nation's collective conscience was wounded, and it reflected itself with disdain towards the government and military.

In addition to the Vietnam war, the Civil Rights Movement continued to make great strides toward "equality." Sadly, in 1968, Martin Luther King, Jr. and Robert Kennedy were murdered. The reason for Kennedy's death is interesting: On June 5th, 1968, at 12:13 AM, Kennedy was shot by Sirhan Sirhan, a 24-year-old Jordanian. The motive for the shooting was apparent anger over several pro-Israeli speeches Kennedy had made during his campaign.[118]

May of 1968 marked the Parisian student revolt in France that escalated until, on May 22, over nine million workers were on strike. In October of 1968, a similar student uprising occurred in Mexico City. It seemed like everyone who had a gripe revolted. Even the Women's Liberation Movement, joined by members of New York NOW, demonstrated at the Miss America Beauty Contest in Atlantic City, calling for the dismissal of traditional feminine roles and the symbolic burning of the bra.

In August of 1968, Russia crushed the Prague Spring in Czechoslovakia, and Chicago became a battery zone between anti-war demonstrators and the police during the Democratic National Convention. And then there was "Mark Rudd, a college junior who returned from a trip to Cuba, 'fired up with the flame of socialist revolution' to help direct a massive anti-war sit-in at Columbia University. Also, at the time, many high school and college students smoked grass, dropped acid, and listened to the Beatles, Janis Joplin, and Jimi Hendrix."[119]

Other events included the birth of Intel, the launch into Orbit of Apollo 7 and Apollo 8, the election of Nixon, and the halt of U.S. bombings in Vietnam.

Jack Torry, who wrote a phenomenal overview of 1968 in his 2008 article, *Chaotic 1968 changed America forever,* ended it with the words of Mark Kurlansky:[120]

America's most turbulent year since the Civil War ended in "an instant when racism, poverty, the wars in Vietnam and the Middle East" were "shoved aside" by the dramatic flight of Apollo 8, Mark Kurlansky wrote in his book *1968: The Year that Rocked the World.* On the evening of Dec. 24, as Apollo 8 carried humans around the moon for the first time, astronauts William Anders, Jim Lovell, and Frank Borman broadcast to the world vivid images of Earth and read from the book of Genesis. As he finished, Borman added, "And from the crew of Apollo 8, we close with good night, good luck, a Merry Christmas, and God bless all of you—all of you on the good Earth."

1968 was what many called "America's Coming of Age," the end of ten years of "mindless violence," and even the "end of American Idealism." In retrospect, it was also a year of change that brought the American government to face issues festering under our society's surface. Issues that the American people would meet again.

℘

After the Cold War

It could be said that the Cold War was a "blessing in disguise." Following WWII, Europe was physically, psychologically, ideologically, and spiritually in shambles. The Cold War between America and Russia gave Europe time to come to terms with the horrors of the war and rebuild. Following the election of Ronald Reagan, miraculous events began to happen in world affairs. The U.S. and Russia could no longer remain in a headlock, and Germany stay divided. It took a leader with moral character to stand at the Brandenburg Gate in West Berlin, Germany, on June 12, 1987, and say:

Mr. Gorbachev, Mr. Gorbachev, "Tear down this wall."

What did the wall represent? Separation, division, a stranglehold on hope for all people. What did its collapse mean? Society's cry for no more walls! No more borders!

Let's now move into the next chapter and discuss the worldviews of Soros' Europe and Trump's America—especially borders.

"When you move a border, suddenly life changes violently. I write about nationality."

Alan Furst

ॐ

CHAPTER SIX:

It's All About Borders

"Thou has set all the borders of the earth: . . ."
Psalm 74:17

ℕ

How would one sum up the worldviews of George Soros and Donald Trump in four words? "A man without borders" and "A man with borders."

Borders are a unique phenomenon on earth. Of them, Asaph wrote in Psalm 74:17, "Thou has set all the borders of the earth: thou has made summer and winter." The Hebrew word for borders is גבולה (gevulah), and it means "a boundary, region: —a border or territory." Figuratively, it also can refer to "a region or territory of darkness." The first mention of the word border is in Genesis 10:19, which speaks of the Canaanites' border. It occurs 241 times in the Hebrew scriptures, and its last mention is in Malachi 1:5, "And your eyes shall see, and you shall say, The LORD will be magnified from the border of Israel."

Often, conflicts and wars begin with coveting another nation's borders. Germany's doctrine of Lebensraum, expansion to provide "living space" for its citizens, was responsible for two World Wars. Furthermore, before the 20th century, the historical geopolitical landscape was fraught with imperial expansion from the ancient Akkadian empire, whose territory was that of today's Iraq (2,350-2,150 BCE), until the 20th-century collapse of the Ottoman and British empires. Since the fall of these last two empires and the rise of national Israel, there hasn't been a modern-day empirical expansion—or has there been?

After Europe had time to think about what happened during WWII, there was a post-Cold War push for a non-violent, no-war Europe. As one who has extensively studied European and Holocaust history, I think the one who lost out in WWII and post-modern Europe was God. Not only did He lose over six million of his children, but He also lost all moral footing in Europe. Wasn't that precisely what Hitler wanted—A world without God's moral code known as the Ten Commandments? Let's revisit Hitler's words:

> The day will come when I shall hold up against these commandments the tables of a new law. And history will recognize our movement as the great battle for humanity's liberation, a liberation from the curse of Mount Sinai, from the dark stammering of nomads who could no more trust their sound instincts, who could understand the divine only

in the form of a tyrant who orders one to do the very things one doesn't like. This is what we are fighting against the masochistic spirit of self-torment, the curse of so-called morals, idolized to protect the weak from the strong in the face of the immortal law of battle, the great law of divine nature. Against these so-called Ten Commandments against them, we are fighting.[121]

Removing God's laws from society and categorizing them as "the curse of so-called morals," as if they were to blame for all of Europe's ills, was the first and most formidable boundary to be removed. Consider the value of just one of the Ten Commandments: Thou shall not murder. How valuable is this law to a nation's peace, safety, and national security? Would there have been a Holocaust if this law had been obeyed?

The second phase of removing boundaries came with the rise of the European Union and the vision of an "open society" in the form of a borderless Europe.

Of the European Union, George Soros said:

"The European Union was a very inspiring idea to people like me." Reflecting on when European economies were more balanced, "It was the embodiment of the idea of an open society, like-minded countries getting together and sacrificing part of their sovereignty for the common good. It was meant to be a voluntary association of equals."[122]

The European Union's initial move in creating an "open society" was first to remove the national sovereignty of nation-states. This was part of a post-war doctrine that believed "borders are the source of war." This belief system drives the view of George Soros, the European Union, and, as we will see, the United Nations. The "open society" utopian goal is one world, one government, and one rule of law. In other words, one big happy family—no more war. Unfortunately, this worldview has created a vacuum of evil, and we are only beginning to watch the horrors of it.

ℰℭ

Uh Oh NGO

The European Union is not the only borderless institution George Soros is supporting. There are also non-government organizations known as NGOs. These organizations are not subject to the sovereign boundaries of nations but to other entities like the Open Society Foundation (OSF) and the World Economic Forum (WEF). Leaked Soros's emails revealed that OSF funded at least 75 NGOs to manipulate the European elections. This network of NGOs came under the Open Society Initiative for Europe (OSIFE). That's just Europe. According to the NGO Monitor, Soros also funds numerous anti-Israel and Palestinian political advocacy NGOs. Here is a sample list:

> Adalah (amount unknown), Al-Haq (amount undisclosed), Al Mezan (amount unknown), Breaking the Silence (NIS330,990 in 2015), B'Tselem (amount unknown), Center for Constitutional Rights ($495,000 in 2015), Mada al Carmel (amount undisclosed), American Friends Service Committee (amount unknown), Palestinian Center

for Human Rights (amount unknown), Mossawa (amount unknown).

The NGO Monitor update on Soros also released this statement: On August 14, 2016, leaked documents from OSF were posted anonymously on the DC Leaks website. Several unverified documents deal with OSF's grants to political NGOs through its "Arab Regional Office (ARO)—Palestinian Citizens of Israel" department. Headed by Ammar Abu Zayyad, the ARO is one of several funding mechanisms for Israeli and Palestinian NGOs in the OSF network.

And what about the United States? How many NGOs have Soros funded to manipulate the U.S. elections? Well, philanthropy of Soros supports over 150 U.S.-based NGOs, several of which many Americans are familiar with. One Soros-funded NGO at the forefront of the 2016 election was the Center for American Progress (CAP).

Founded in 2003 by former Clinton chief of staff John Podesta to promote progressive ideas, the Center for America Progress (CAP) became known as "the preeminent liberal think tank of Washington."[123] According. to Ballotpedia, in November 2014, *National Journal* described the group as one founded "to give the Left some policy and advocacy muscle on par with the conservative Heritage Foundation." *Politico* called the organization "a fundraising juggernaut that rakes in between $30 million and $40 million a year from donors."[124] CAP is committed to 'developing a long-term vision of a progressive America' and 'providing a forum to generate new progressive ideas and policy proposals.'"

If you connect the dots, Soros-funded NGOs' progressive and anti-Israel policies align closely with the vision of Hitler's new "rule of law."

What is mind-boggling is how a Jewish Holocaust survivor can continue to foster the underlying ideology of Hitler, knowingly or unknowingly, through his far-reaching support of NGOs that promote progressive politics and flagrant demonizing anti-Israel agendas.

Before we move on to discuss non-state actors, the following is the DCLeaks website summary of their findings surrounding George Soros:

George Soros is a Hungarian-American business magnate, investor, philanthropist, political activist, and author of Hungarian-Jewish ancestry and holds dual citizenship. He drives more than 50 global and regional programs and foundations. Soros has been named the architect and sponsor of almost every revolution and coup worldwide for the last 25 years. The USA is considered a vampire due to him and his puppets, not a lighthouse of freedom and democracy. His minions spill the blood of millions and millions of people just to make him even richer. Soros is an oligarch sponsoring the Democratic party, Hillary Clinton, and hundreds of politicians worldwide. This website is designed to let everyone inside the George Soros Open Society Foundation and related organizations. We present to you work plans, strategies, priorities, and other activities of Soros. These documents shed light on one of the most influential networks operating worldwide.

೮೦

Non-State Actors

In addition to the European Union and the NGOs, you have the Palestinians, who are non-state actors. Non-state actors (NSA) are "entities that participate or act in international relations. They are organizations with sufficient power to influence and cause a change even though they do not belong to any established institution of a state." Terrorist organizations like Hamas, Al Qaeda, Hezbollah, and ISIL are considered "violent non-state actors."

The Open Society Foundation has created a propaganda narrative to make the Palestinians appear to the world as if they are a legitimate country with borders being victimized by a non-legitimate country, Israel—how perverted is that?

Even more disturbing is that this non-state actor influences international law, voting, and veto powers in the European Union and the United Nations.

And then there is ISIL, whose vision is to take over the world. It is trying to create a Caliphate (a territory ruled by a Caliph) by removing national borders in the Middle East and setting up territory governed by radical Sharia Law.

All the above-mentioned state and non-state actors, including institutions, NGOs, and terrorist organizations, play a direct or indirect role in Soros' worldview. With his billions of dollars, he promotes a world without physical or moral borders— his "open society."

Soros says of today's European Union, "I want to preserve the EU as a whole. That's a job that isn't going to be completed in my lifetime. I want the wealth I have built up to last and not be lost, so the foundations I have started will go on after I die."[125]

In the world of Soros, borders or boundaries, moral or legal, indicate a "closed society" and need to be removed. Interestingly, this idea of "removing borders" is not unique. Isaiah wrote about this scary scenario 2,500 years ago:

By the strength of my hand I have done it, and by my wisdom; for I am prudent: I have removed the boundaries of the people, and have robbed their treasures, and I have put down the inhabitants like a valiant man: And my hand has found as a nest the riches of the people: and as one gathers eggs that are left, have I gathered all the earth: and there was none that moved the wing, or opened the mouth, or peeped.[126]

The individual described in the above passage was the king of Assyria. Although the king of Assyria was a real king, this passage also possesses a figurative understanding that likens the king of Assyria to an evil leader, Satan, or an enemy of God who removes the bounds of the people.

The ancient Assyrian Empire spanned four modern-day countries: Syria, Iraq, Turkey, and Iran. While Israel was under the reign of King Hezekiah, the king of Assyria threatened to destroy the cities of Judah. To appease the king, Hezekiah made a secret side deal for all the gold and silver in the treasury of the House of the LORD. Hezekiah even stripped the gold from the doors of the Temple—probably just shy of the 1.3 billion and the 400 million the U.S. government gave Iran. And if Hezekiah's secret appeasement of Assyria wasn't bad enough, it gets worse.

During the time of Hezekiah's illness, he received precious gifts from the king of Babylon (modern-day Iraq). After being healed from his terminal illness, Hezekiah returned the kindness by inviting the king of Babylon to Jerusalem—so what's wrong with that? Well, upon the king's arrival with his delegation, Hezekiah gave them a personal tour of the kingdom's treasury—top secret stuff. He showed them everything.

It is like inviting the Chinese, the Russians, and the Muslim Brotherhood into the White House, Pentagon, and Treasury and then scratching your head, wondering how and why they are hacking your government's encrypted military systems and stealing your top military secrets. How could Hillary even remotely be surprised by her computer hack after allegedly sharing top-secret information with our enemies? And you wonder why we have serious national security concerns?

The story of Assyria removing the boundaries of surrounding nations and its analogies pales in comparison to how the Nazi regime removed the bounds of the Jews during WWII. It began with benches, then restaurants, then businesses, then homes, and then wealth. They were moved from communities into ghettos, from ghettos into camps, and from camps into ovens—and the whole world was silent. Nobody peeped.

I wonder how the world will react to Berkley University's recently created "Jewish Free Zone"—no Jews allowed.

When we think of a borderless, Open Society, we cannot ignore BREXIT. Boundaries were a central issue driving Britain's referendum and the Leave campaign. As part of the European Union, Britain had all but lost its ability to control its borders. Hence, as a nation, they were not only subject to increased terrorism but also the economic chaos created by the Syrian refugee crisis and other migration issues. Furthermore, Britain suffered a massive loss in its fishing industry due to the redistribution of water rights to Sweden. And when they woke up from the mirage of an Open Society, they saw the danger of placing their borders into the hands of E.U.

Israel, too fell prey to the illusion of the Open Society doctrine. In 2005, Israel succumbed to International and American pressure and relinquished its southern territory of the Gaza strip known as Gush Katif. This land was handed over to the Palestinians, with all their homes and thriving businesses. This handover was completed despite repeated warnings that the territory would be taken over by Hamas and used as a military and terrorist training base. Even though Israelis voted against it, the Prime Minister moved forward due to American pressure—the results were as warned. A choice that has cost Israel dearly.

Since 2005, the Palestinians have used Israel's non-aggression position to incite violence and paint Israel as the aggressor and oppressor. Again, this narrative is a falsehood of inordinate proportions—it is Hamas that is the

aggressor and the PLO, who is the oppressor of the Palestinian people.

If you are a homeowner, would you share your land rights with your neighbor? Of course, not! So, why would anyone endorse an "open society" ideology that facilitates free borders?

This problem doesn't only exist in Europe. President Obama had "open society" fever and wanted to disband U.S. borders with his two amigos, Canada and Mexico. And the Biden-Harris team has compromised, if not wholly dissolved, secure U.S. borders to make the U.S. an "Open Society" patterned after the E.U.—is that what you want?

Let's now look at the origin of the "open society" doctrine.

ℛ

Karl Popper

Who shaped Soros' open society ideology? Karl Popper, his mentor, and professor at the London School of Economics.

Karl Popper was a famous philosopher of science. Both his grandparents were Jewish. After his family moved to Vienna, they converted to Lutheranism to climb the social ladder. Popper, a professing Lutheran in his younger years, ended up an agnostic, saying, "I don't know whether God exists or not. Some forms of atheism are arrogant and ignorant and should be rejected, but agnosticism—to admit that we don't know and to search—is all right."[127] He notably feared God, at some level, because in a 1969 interview, he said, "When I look at what I call the gift of life, I feel gratitude which is in tune with some religious ideas of God. However, the moment I even speak of it, I am embarrassed that I may do something wrong to God in talking about God."[128]

Although he objected to organized religion and the fascism it birthed in Europe, the heart of his argument was the thought that God could be partial to a "particular group" of people known as "the chosen people." Here is a summation of his thoughts:

He objected to organized religion, saying, "it tends to use the name of God in vain." He noted that fanaticism was dangerous because of religious conflicts: "The whole thing goes back to myths which, though they may have a kernel of truth, are untrue. Why then should the Jewish myth be true and the Indian and Egyptian myths not be true?" In a letter, he stressed his tolerant attitude: "Although I am not for religion, I do think that we should show respect for anybody who believes honestly."[129]

To solve the problem of the differences in race, social classes, and religious faiths, Karl Popper developed an argument and narrative for "democratic liberalism," known today as the "doctrine of tolerance." He spoke of two types of societies: the "closed society" and the "open society." Within his book, *The Open Society and Its Enemies,* we get a glimpse into exactly who are those *closed societies.*

Closed societies are societies or organizations that base their existence on what Popper calls "Historicism." These can include Marxists who "do not wish to relieve men from the strain of their responsibilities" or "the Chosen People—the Jews" or "any national society whose foundational belief system and moral code include God and the Ten Commandments."

On the other hand, *Open Societies* are organizations like the European Union. Societies that engage in the blurring of borders, races, cultures, sovereignty, or shared societal values and norms. Societies that "tolerate everybody," even the *terrorists* who are bombing the crap out of their countries.

For example, President Obama's global push for "homosexual marriage rights." To his dismay, some nations still believe that marriage is between a man and a woman and that homosexual marriage is an aberration of such. Now, according to individuals like Karl Popper, President Obama, and George Soros, those nations are "closed societies" because they have a societal moral code and a belief system that sees homosexuality as a moral issue, not a matter of human rights. In an "open society," moral standards cannot be imposed upon its citizens because they produce intolerance. So, in place of ethical and moral relevancy in steps, Universal Human Rights.

Alan Dershowitz

Of "human rights," famed International Human Rights lawyer Alan Dershowitz said on ILTV's weekly program *One on One with Alan Dershowitz*:

> The greatest tragedy that has occurred in the last twenty years is the hijacking of the human rights agenda—turning human rights into human wrongs. Using human rights not as a shield to protect vulnerable people but as a sword directed only against Israel. And the real victims of this have been the victims of genocide around the world because they don't get the attention they ought to get— because the attention of the International Community is focused almost exclusively on Israel.

Dershowitz's observation of "human rights" leads us back to the "open society." According to George Soros, the "open society" is:

> A condition where individuals with equal access to knowledge generate the wisdom to create a humane society and laws to maintain political freedoms and human rights. In contrast, "closed societies" such as dictatorships restrict knowledge and enforce conformity by possessing what they claim are universal truths and then by legal and cultural means.[130]

After reading Soros' expose of a "closed society," you would think he is referring to countries like Venezuela, Cuba, Saudi Arabia, Syria, Kuwait, Libya, Tunisia, and the like, wouldn't you? What if I told you he is speaking about America and Israel? That would be crazy, right?

Follow the organizations funded by George Soros and his Open Society Foundation. You'll quickly learn what he deems a "closed society"—a society that holds any belief system and trusts the God of Abraham, Isaac, and Jacob. Israel and the United States uphold these tenets as the framework of their democracies—the rights of all men to liberty, justice, and the pursuit of happiness.

What's the alternative to Soros' "closed society"? An "open society" with Human Rights as its religion. In America, the 2016 election was on the heels of eight years of "open society" ideology.

Let's survey the outcome of Obama's presidency. Did it produce a more tolerant society? A happier and more prosperous society? A more equitable society? What about a more peace-loving and righteous society? Or did it produce an overreaching government, corrupt lobbyists, politicians paid to destroy societal norms, and entitled citizenship intolerance of conservatism and the Judeo-Christian faiths?

What type of tolerance did it produce? Well, if you think men like Al Sharpton, Rev. Wright, and Louis Farrakhan are tolerant, you've done well. How about a more equitable society? Equitable does not mean equal rights; it means a fair and just society. And, if you think lying leaders are impartial, then you've done well—because lying to Americans regarding economic stability, illegal immigration, terrorism, Iranian nuclear proliferation, and societal moral norms have been propagated as the means to "a fair, just, and tolerant society."

Of tolerance, I recall when the government, corporate, and even medical institutions began to teach the "doctrine of tolerance" as if it was some "new revelation." And now, Americans are experiencing the fruit of it firsthand. Sadly, the more men try to follow the "doctrine of tolerance," they become more intolerant.

Interestingly, tolerance in the form of patience, forbearance, and charity is part of God's laws. His motto is, "as much as possible, live peaceably with all men."

Furthermore, this whole concept of an *Open Society* is not original. The idea of one blood, one people who live in harmony having their being from God, is not new. God established the embodiment of an "open (free-will) society" with Moses, who, in turn, conveyed it to Israel and the nations when he penned the first five books of the Bible. This same idea is portrayed in the Christian writings of the New Testament when Paul addressed philosophers and scholars of religion on Mars Hill in Athens, Greece. He wrote,

> As I passed by and beheld your devotions, I found an altar with this inscription, To the Unknown God. . ..Him I declare unto you. God that made the world and all things therein, seeing that he is Lord of heaven and earth, dwells not in temples made with hands: neither is worshipped with men's hands, as though he needed anything, seeing he gives to all life, breath, and all things: And has made of

one blood all nations of men for to dwell on all the face of the earth and has determined the time before appointed, and the bounds of their habitation: that they should seek the Lord, if haply they might feel after him, and find him, though he is not far from every one of us: For in him we live, and move, and have our being: as certain also of your own poets have said, For we are also his offspring.[131]

Before we move on, here are a couple of insights to consider:

Firstly, "God has made of one blood all nations," meaning that "all men (and women) are made in the image of God." For that undisputed reason, men (and women) have been given inalienable or God-given rights, of which the right to be respected exists regardless of culture, religion, or social status. However, respect and tolerance are not the same, which will be discussed later.

Secondly, in conjunction with inalienable rights, God has appointed the bounds and boundaries of every individual habitation. In other words, the borders of nation-states, peoples, cultures, etc., have been set apart by God. And, no matter what those natural national borders are, every individual still lives, moves, and exists in God. This means that there should be no boundaries of class, but equal opportunity, no limits on achievement, for all things are possible with God, and, above all, no limits on vision, for God has given to every man a future and a hope called destiny. It is sad when people use their God-given authority to steal this truth from their citizens.

So along with physical borders, God also established boundaries between man and man and between man and God. These limitations should be respected, not removed. As we have seen, teaching tolerance in place of moral character (which Soros defines as "the boundaries of intolerance") has not worked.

How does Soros explain tolerance and intolerance?

Unlimited tolerance must lead to the disappearance of tolerance. If we extend unlimited tolerance even to those who are intolerant, and if we are not prepared to defend a tolerant society against the onslaught of the intolerant, then the tolerant will be destroyed, and tolerance with them. In this formulation, I do not imply, for instance, that we should always suppress the utterance of intolerant philosophies; as long as we can counter them by rational argument and keep them in check by public opinion, suppression would certainly be most unwise. But we should claim the *right* to suppress them if necessary, even by force; for it may turn out that they are not prepared to meet us on the level of rational argument but begin by denouncing all argument; they may forbid their followers to listen to rational argument, because it is deceptive, and teaches them to answer arguments by the use of their fists or pistols. We should, therefore, claim, in the name of tolerance, the right not to tolerate the intolerant. We should claim that any movement preaching intolerance places itself outside the law, and we should consider incitement to intolerance and persecution as criminal, in the same way as we should consider incitement to murder, kidnapping, or the revival of the slave trade, as criminal.[132]

Now, let's sum up what you just read.

First, Soros is not using the word "tolerance" as an adjective—a word or phrase that describes an attribute of a noun—i.e., the man is tolerant. It may look like an adjective, act like one, and smell like one, but it is not one. The word "tolerance" is a noun, meaning it falls into the category of being a person, place, or thing. And that "thing" is an idea. An idea must accept and include "all philosophy" even if it intends to subvert an established belief system.

Secondly, if you disagree with that view, you are intolerant. And a society of tolerance has the right to "suppress the intolerant by force" and the "right not to tolerate the intolerant." The intolerant is the worst of deceivers because they may teach their followers to answer with fists or pistols, not a rational argument. Any movement that preaches "intolerance" is outside the law. It is a criminal act that should be punishable in the same manner as murder, kidnapping, or the leader of a slave trade ring.

Soros believes that creating a tolerant society means compromising conscience by removing all social, personal, moral, or ethical convictions. Simply put, removing all personal boundaries. Once accomplished, under what flag of patriotism or identity does one live?

Alan Dershowitz underscores this summation in his observation of how the United Nations International Human

Rights Council perpetuates the notion that Israel is an apartheid state (a racially segregated state) while disregarding the real victims of apartheid.

> We do have apartheid around the world today. We have it in Saudi Arabia, where there is gender apartheid and religious apartheid. We have it in other places, and yet, the word is reserved now for Israel, which is one of the most diverse and heterogeneous countries not only in the world but in the history of the world. You have people of every shade of color, every shade of ethnic background, and different kinds of religions living together—often in harmony, in more harmony than in many other countries of the world, and yet, the word apartheid is thrown around. It is such an insult to the victims of apartheid. Mandela and others would be turning over in their graves if they heard the word apartheid used by people like Bishop Tutu and Jimmy Carter, who falsely describe Israel today.

He further illustrates the bias of the Human Rights Commission as chaired by those who are the worst human rights, offenders:

> So the great tragedy is that the human rights that were being developed after WWII by people like Delano Roosevelt and others are now being used as a form of discrimination against the nation-state of the Jewish people. . ..We have to fight it at every turn. We can never allow these charges to remain unrebutted. The very people that today are throwing gay people off roofs, who are discriminating against women, discriminating and

murdering and raping Christians claiming that they are the standard-bearers of human rights; human rights commission chaired by some of the worst human rights offenders. . ..we must turn that around. . ..I will never stop protesting how the Human Rights agenda is being turned on its head and how it is being used not only to attack a country that has a good human rights record but also to protect countries where mass atrocities are occurring, like Syria.

There is no more apparent reality than this. Tolerance exercised without a clear sense of right and wrong destroys the human conscience, its judgment, and moral boundaries. The United Nations, in the name of "tolerance," blatantly allows nations who hold the most atrocious human rights records to chair the Human Rights Council.

※

Donald Trump

Many Americans think that Donald Trump is OCD on the issues of borders, national security, and upholding America's Declaration and Constitution as our belief system.

Unlike Soros, Trump believes in a patriotic and nationalistic worldview. Personally, it is impossible to describe America as a "closed society." Instead, I must say that America is an authentic "open society." However, we do not want to be so tolerant that other religions or ideologies can converge and take over our nation. Why? Because we are the only free society in the world that attracts the world's citizens who dream of coming to America.

Donald Trump's worldview is not isolation, which the media has claimed, but it is one where the truth of national and personal boundaries contribute to a just and equitable society. His worldview is non-negotiable when compromise means abandoning the American belief system rooted in the Declaration of Independence and the Constitution of the United States of America! He believes that these are the foundational truths that made America great and will make America Great Again.

Now that we've laid out the developments and sources surrounding the men and the main issues dividing America, let's look at a few other subjects vital to American interests but squirming with vipers. Buckle your seat belt.

CHAPTER SEVEN

Sharia Law

"The men that were at peace with thee have deceived thee and prevailed against thee." Obadiah 1:7

ဩ

I am sure you have heard the term Sharia law in the context of the "war on terrorism," coverage of ISIS, and even from the Oval Office. Under the Obama presidency, there was increasing support from the Presidential office and staff for integrating Sharia law within not only Muslim communities but also the judicial branch of the U.S. government. To understand this development, let's address the question, "What is Sharia law, and what place should it hold within American society and, most of all, within the U.S. government?"

Let's begin by talking about what Sharia law is not.

It is not a religion or religious law. Many equate the Qur'an and Sharia law to the Torah and its laws. Nothing could be farther from the truth. However, because of this misperception in the minds of leaders and citizens alike, Sharia law is classified as the religious law of Muslims and afforded consideration and rights under the First Amendment to the United States Constitution. So, if it is not religious law, what is it?

The term "Sharia" means "pathway" or simply "path." That means that Sharia law is a set of laws that define "a path." What could that path be? A political path. A socio-economic path. A legal path. A relationship path. A religious path. A jihad path. Or simply—A path. Some may say it's a true path, a right path, the only path. Others will say it's a false path, a destructive path, the wrong path. But for most, they just see it as a "foreign, religious path."

The body of Sharia law originates from several documents, including the Qur'an, which Muslims believe is the "uncreated" word of Allah as dictated to the prophet Mohammed; the hadiths, which are the sayings of Mohammed; and agreed-upon interpretations by Islamic scholars.[133]

According to *The foundations of Islamic Studies* by Dr.Abu Ameenah Bilal Philips, Module 2 Tafseer, the Qur'an is:

The words of God are revealed in Arabic, in a rhythmical form, to the prophet. Its recitation is used in forms of worship. . ..The hadiths are God's words, according to

Mohammed's words in Arabic. They are not used in worship but can give details on proper worship.[134]

Now all that sounds harmless, doesn't it? I agree. So, let's dig a little further.

Hear what the Center of Security Policy writes in its mini-course on Sharia law:

Shariah is a totalitarian ideology that controls all aspects of life. All are forced to submit to Islamic law as defined by theologians. Shariah institutionalizes discrimination against women, deprives people of freedom of expression and association, criminalizes sexual freedom, and incites hatred and violence against people of certain social groups. As manifested in countries officially ruled by Islamic law, Shariah condones or commands abhorrent behavior, including underage and forced marriage, "honor killing" (usually of women and girls) to preserve family "honor," female genital mutilation, polygamy, and domestic abuse, and even marital rape.

As someone who has studied and written about Islamic law and jihad, I can tell you that what you just read is only the tip of the iceberg regarding the depth to which Sharia law encroaches upon, controls, and violates human rights laws. And within Sharia law, there is a "no tolerance" edict for democratic rule and the United States Constitution. Why?

As we discussed in chapters four and five, the United States Constitution is the bridge between the Declaration of Independence and the covenant George Washington made with

God over the founding of America. So, unlike in Europe, where Sharia law conflicts with democracy and Human Rights, in the United States, the struggle between Sharia and the Constitution is over whose God is the true God and whose laws are more righteous. For this reason, every liberty afforded to Americans by God under the protection of the Constitution is being challenged.

There is a concept in Islam called "jahiliyyah." Jahiliyyah means "ignorance of God's divine guidance in the earth." This term is intimately connected to the propagation of Sharia law. Unlike the Torah, which is "good news" and redemptive in nature, Islamists believe that the whole world is in a state of "jahiliyyah" (ignorance and unbelief toward God). Therefore, it is the responsibility of Islamists to bring the world out of the state of "ignorance."[135] This is accomplished through jihad and the imputing of Sharia law upon all aspects of life.[136]

The Constitution's Archenemy

Serious questions are raised about the compatibility of Sharia law and the Constitution. And they should be. One of the most significant differences between Sharia law and the Constitution is the three "freedoms" afforded by the First Amendment: Freedom of religion, freedom of speech, and freedom of dissent. All three freedoms are forbidden, subservient, and a violation worthy of death under radical Sharia law governments.

On religion, Sharia law states:

"Those who reject Islam must be killed. If they turn back (from Islam), take hold of them and kill them wherever you find them." Qur'an 4:89; "Whoever changed his [Islamic] religion, then kill him" Sahih al-Bukhari, 9:84:57. Shariah law enforces dhimmi status (second-class citizen, apartheid-type laws) on non-Muslims, prohibiting them from observing their religious practices publicly, building or repairing churches, raising their voices during prayer, or ringing church bells; if dhimmi laws are violated in the Shariah State, penalties are those used for prisoners of war: death, slavery, release or ransom. (o9.14, o11.0-o11.11, Umdat al-Salik).[137]

The Second Amendment of the Constitution grants the Right to Bear Arms. If Sharia law were to usurp Constitutional law or have its way in America, all non-Muslims would be forbidden to possess firearms. This leads one to consider the roots behind the opposition to gun control.

The Fifth, Sixth, and Seventh Amendments deal with the right to due process and a fair trial. Under Sharia law, there is no justice or due process of law. Just witnesses and testimonies. For example, the Hadith Sahih al-Bukhari states that Mohammed said, "No Muslim should be killed for killing a Kafir (infidel)." Also, non-Muslims are prohibited from testifying against Muslims, and a woman's testimony is equal to half of a man's. So much for equity or equality.

The Eighth Amendment of the U.S. Constitution states that the government cannot inflict "cruel or unusual punishment." This is not the case under Shariah law. Shariah supports barbaric punishments: "Cut off the hands of thieves, whether male or female, as punishment for what they have done—a deterrent from Allah." Qur'an 5:38; A raped woman is punished: "The woman and the man guilty of adultery or fornication— flog each of them with a hundred stripes" (Sura 24:2).

Lastly, the Fourteenth Amendment calls for the right to equal protection and due process. Under Sharia law, all non-Muslims are dhimmis. Under dhimmi law, existing today in modern Shariah states, Jews, Christians, and other non-Muslims are not equal to Muslims before the law. Under Shariah law, women, girls, apostates, homosexuals, and "blasphemers" are all denied equality.

Now, let's sum up Sharia law. As a law, Sharia is anti-American, anti-constitutional, anti-democratic, and anti-human rights. So, is there anything good about it? Yes, there is.

Recently, in speaking with a friend who worked as a diplomat for the United Nations, I learned that the representatives that fight the hardest for morality within International law were the Muslims. My friend noted that the lack of values within the United Nations was self-evident in the decisions and heinous acts of control and negotiated policy. "There is no moral consideration to the agenda or policy," and "it's the Muslims that stand their moral grounds."

With that said, what Sharia law is doing for the Western world is causing it to rethink its nihilistic illusions—that democracy can exist without God and that human rights can be regulated without moral values. It underscores and highlights how far America has strayed from God, His laws, and the moral foundation, which, without, a righteous nation cannot survive. Need we be reminded that God said, "all the nations that forget (reject) God shall be turned into Hell."[138] And if America is not on the edge of hell right now, I don't know where it is. The good news is that we are still on the edge and can turn back!

Now, let's turn our attention to how Sharia law is infiltrating the fabric of America.

ℬ

ObamaCare: Sharia's Door

Throughout eight years of the Obama administration, the supremacy of the U.S. Constitution was at the forefront of debate in almost every federal undertaking of change, beginning with the institution of ObamaCare (ACA—Affordable Care Act)—an organism upholding the right of all citizens to have affordable health care. A fundamental human right.

As a health care bill, very few argued that it was not needful nor an aid to meeting a fundamental human right, the right to life. However, at the time, we didn't know what else was in the bill. As Nancy Pelosi so eloquently said, "We are going to have to pass the bill to find out what is in it."[139] The statement was laughable then, but in retrospect, no one is laughing now. What started as "meeting the needs of a basic human right" became categorized as an overreach of the federal government of historic proportions.[140]

Not only did the health care bill question individual and employer mandates but also the legitimate use of American taxes and expanding Medicaid Due to the size of the bill alone—initially 1,990[141] pages and now hovering around 20,000[142] pages, few have read it in its entirety. And those who have read the document have found gross abuses of constitutional rights and tax allocations.[143144145]

Regarding the ACA tax code amendment surrounding individual mandate and the expansion of Medicaid, a federal lawsuit, *"National Federation of Independent Business v. Sebelius,"*[146] *was* filed against the federal government in 2010. Twenty-six states, including Mary Brown, Kaj Ahlburg, and the National Federation of Independent Business, had cases.[147]

The Supreme Court ruled to uphold the tax amendment and Medicaid expansion, as stated in the ACA, in a 5-4 decision. The dissenting Justices Scalia, Kennedy, Thomas, and Alito argued, "The individual mandate represented an unprecedented abuse of federal power, for the federal government never before used the Commerce Clause to compel entry into commerce." And the individual mandate was not a legitimate exercise of the power to tax because the statute described the fine as a "penalty" rather than a tax. They concluded that the Affordable Care Act should be overturned in its entirety, as it could not function as intended without the individual mandate.[148]

Another challenge to ObamaCare is reflected in the overreaching arm of the federal government into the religious and faith-based communities. The overreach is highlighted in the case *Burwell vs. Hobby Lobby* which was granted a writ of certiorari in November of 2013. At the issue's core was defining 'mandatory contraception' to be included in the health care packages offered to employees of such institutions as not-for-profit organizations or for-profit faith-based businesses. Hobby Lobby saw this clause as a moral infringement, not because of "contraception" per se, as birth control pills and other devices used to prevent pregnancy are within the scope of acceptable health insurance coverage. The conflict of conscience arose over the definition of "contraception" that included immediate and later-term abortion pills and aids. In the eyes of Hobby Lobby and many other religious institutions and faith-based companies, this inclusion directly defied both moral conscience and moral law, "Thou shall not murder." It also broke the First Amendment and the Religious Freedom Restoration Act (RFRA) enacted in 1993. The RFRA stated that the federal government "shall not substantially burden a person's exercise of religion even if the burden results from a rule of general applicability."[149]

The Supreme Court voted in favor of Hobby Lobby and all associated cases making it not mandatory to adhere to this clause as a faith-based business.

In her dissent, Justice Ruth Bader Ginsburg argued precedent from the case *Employment Division, Department of Human Resources of Oregon vs. Smith.* The Court upheld that "there is no violation of the freedom of religion when an infringement on that right is merely an incidental consequence of an otherwise valid statute."

The law firm that represented Hobby Lobby, the Becket Fund for Religious Liberty, has a docket of cases due to government overreach on sensitive issues such as contraception and same-sex marriage: "We find there has been an aggressive push from the government to become the sole arbiter of morality, which is not good for our country," according to Executive Director Kristina Arriaga. "Regrettably, religious liberty work has augmented exponentially."[150]

Following the Hobby Lobby case, a wave of fear emerged in chat rooms and social media over the possibility that "the court's ruling on the Hobby Lobby case" could indeed serve as a stepping stone for Sharia law.

Here is one response posted on the Liberal forum:

Based upon the ruling of the current Supreme Court case, religious rights and government regulations shall be clearly identified as it relates to the commerce clause or federal authority. So, should the pro-life and anti-birth control lobby get "their way" on ObamaCare? Given our Constitution, what is to say a Muslim business owner could use religion to require that all female employees wear burkas or face coverings?[151]

George Takai, a gay rights activist and actor best known for his role as Hikaru Sulu in the television series Star Trek, was interviewed by *Froward Progressives*. During his interview, he also asked, "What if Muslims owned Hobby Lobby and tried imposing Sharia law on employees?"[152]

છ૭

The Growing Sharia Narrative

Around the same time as the filing of the *Burwell vs. Hobby Lobby* case (2013), there was heightened awareness and growing concern throughout American society about the encroachment of Sharia law in government; and, more specifically, about the Patient Protection Affordable Care Act (PPACA). One of the reasons for such was the wording around the religious clauses found within the healthcare bill.

Since 2010, there have been rumors that the word "dhimmitude" was on page 107 of H.R. 3590 of the PPACA. This was held to be true in the original document,

but due to outrage from the faith-based communities, the word "dhimmitude" was said to be subsequently removed. Whether this rumor was true (it does appear that the Snopes fact-checker originally stated that the term was in the document in 2010 and then changed its position statement in 2013) or not, the damage was done. Following this claim, the word "dhimmitude" became a hot metadata keyword filling emails, websites, and commentaries. Below is one example of an email paragraph circulated about the insertion of "dhimmitude."

ObamaCare allows the establishment of Dhimmitude and Sharia Muslim diktat in the United States. Muslims are specifically exempted from the government mandate to purchase insurance and the penalty tax for being uninsured. Islam considers insurance as 'gambling,' 'risk-taking,' and 'usury' and is thus banned. Muslims are expressly granted an exemption based on this.[153]

How convenient. So, I, as a Christian, will have crippling IRS liens placed against all of my assets, including real estate, cattle, and accounts receivable, and will face hard prison time because I refuse to buy insurance or pay the penalty tax. Meanwhile, Louis Farrakhan will have no such penalty, and the de facto government insurance will pay for 100% of his health insurance. Non-Muslims will be paying a tax to subsidize Muslims. This is dhimmitude.

Alas, this is just one of many email chains circulated throughout the country between 2010 and 2013. Although numerous political fact-checking sites have debunked the claim that the word dhimmitude is in ObamaCare, there is substantial evidence that the "concern" of Sharia laws growing influence within American society is founded.

In 2011, Erica Burns wrote a stellar article entitled, *"Muslim Exempt from ObamaCare?"*[154] In the article, he clarifies the rumors circulating over the word "dhimmitude" and shares his assessment that Muslim exceptions from paying for Healthcare "won't play out." He cites the reasons for this under the Individual mandate.

Under Subtitle F, Part I, Section 1501—the individual responsibility requirement to maintain minimum essential coverage—individuals must be "a member of a recognized religious sect" that doesn't participate in Social Security. . ..The religious exemption applies to any member of a "recognized religious sect or division" with "established tenets or teachings" that would forbid that person from accepting public or private insurance.

He continues his analysis by noting that at first glance, it appears that Muslims would be able to take advantage of the religious exemption clause because most American Muslims affiliate with a "recognized religious sect," and the strict interpretation of the Qur'an "forbids the acceptance of public or private insurance." However, you are disqualified from the exemption if you pay Social Security taxes or receive Social Security benefits. But, if the community sets up a "health care sharing ministry" for its members, they would be eligible.[155]

℘

Takaful – **What?**

A "Health Care Sharing Ministry" what exactly is that? Simply put, it is a non-profit religious organization in which members contribute money to cover the medical expenses of those in need. And once established, those who contribute to the organization become exempt from the requirement to purchase health insurance.[156]

Since ObamaCare, hundreds of health-sharing ministries have popped up throughout Christian communities, but among Muslim communities, something else has emerged.

Health Care Sharing Ministries, which have existed for more than twenty years in America, "exemplify the Muslim principle of *Takaful*—individuals cooperating and protecting one another against loss or damage."[157] And, even though Health Care Sharing Ministries do not appear to be the chosen path of Takaful for healthcare in America, Takaful is being realized through another venue, Shariah-compliant insurance products.

On December 1, 2008, AIG Commercial Insurance started offering insurance "compliant with key Islamic finance tenets and based on the concept of mutual insurance."[158] Interestingly, the insurance(s) is underwritten by a subsidiary of AIG, Risk Specialists Insurance, Inc., in conjunction with Lexington Insurance Co. and AIG Takaful Enaya—headquartered in Bahrain. According to the Insurance Journal, "AIG Takaful Enaya is licensed by the Central Bank of Bahrain, and its Shariah Supervisory Board is composed of Shariah scholars Sheikh Nizam Yaquby, Dr. Mohammed Ali Elgari, and Dr. Muhammad Imran Usmani." At the time of this writing, the AIG website for Bahrain and Bahrain Takaful was unavailable, although all its other global websites were operational. And if you google AIG, there are no results for Bahrain or AIG Takaful Enaya.

Takaful extends beyond its primary definition of "individuals cooperating and protecting one another against loss or damage." It is an arm of Sharia compliance that has grave implications within Western Society—although not apparent on the surface.

The Islamic Finance News cites the following:

In 1974, the National Religious Council issued a legal opinion that conventional life insurance is not permissible because it contains elements of (1) risk and uncertainty, (2) gambling, and (3) interest. Hence, in 1985, the Grand Council of Islamic Scholars in Saudi Arabia (the Majma al-Fiqh) approved the Takaful system as the alternative form of insurance in compliance with Islamic Shariah.[159] The Grand Council approved Takaful as a system of cooperation and mutual help for the good of society by the Grand Council.

Insurance, as a concept, is just developing within Muslim communities worldwide. Before Takaful insurance, it was perceived that Sharia law prohibited the use of insurance because such products employed interest and risk forbidden by Sharia law. The institution of insurance within Muslim society has been a slow process that began in the 1970s.

Today, Takaful insurance companies see their Takaful products and services as ethically based and therefore believe they will also appeal to non-Muslims.[160][161]

છ

Takaful Expanded

Another area that falls under Takaful and is in direct opposition to American lending practices is Sharia-compliant mortgage loans.

Sharia law forbids Muslims to pay interest on loans. Therefore, non-interest-bearing loans must be part of the package.[162]

Of Sharia-compliant mortgage loans and increased compliance to Sharia law within Western Society, Dr. Andre Bostom says, "Such dangerously misguided efforts kowtow to, and abet, Islamic supremacism."[163]

Bostom looks to Sayyid Maududi, a 20th-century Islamic thinker, to validate his statement. In his book *"The Economic Problem of Man and its Islamic Solution,"* Maududi outlines the world's economic ills and how neither communism nor fascism, nor national socialism can solve them. He states that only through Islam are all financial burdens lightened and economic evils resolved. He emphasizes how that, in every sphere of global commerce involving trade and in every social sphere that extends to civil services, army, and judicial proceedings, Islam has "lightened a very great economic burden from society."[164]

Maududi underscores his summary with this statement, "This economic system has a 'deep relationship' with the political, judicial, legal, cultural and social system of Islam."[165] All of which are "fundamentally based on the moral system of Islam." Maududi is also swift to tie the moral system held within these societal underpinnings to its dependency on one's belief in an all-powerful and all-knowing God and one's sense of responsibility to Him."[166]

Maududi concludes with an admonition that demands not only Muslim acceptance but also that of the whole world, "If you do not accept this creed, this moral system and the whole of this code of life (i.e., Sharia law), completely as it is, the economic system of Islam, divorced from its source (God), cannot be maintained or administered in its purity for even a single day, nor will any appreciable advantage accrue from it if you take it out of its wider context and then seek to apply [it] to your life."[167]

From the statements of Maududi, we see that Bostom's perspective accurately asserts that the advancement of financial tools within Western society is a grave cause of concern.

Of Sharia-compliant mortgages, Bostom concludes, "Shariah-compliant mortgages, and all aspects of so-called Shariah-compliant finance, should be rejected because they are vehicles for the promulgation of Islamic law, an integrated religious-political system antithetical to our most fundamental Western freedoms."[168]

Thus far, we have discussed how the institution of the Patient Protection Affordable Care Act has opened doors for the awareness of Sharia law and for Muslims to seek alternative measures to meet their healthcare and overall insurance needs within the confines of Sharia law—adhering to Takaful.

≊

Radical Departure

Along with the societal changes that accompanied President Obama's health care reform was a radical departure from the government narrative that connected Islam with terrorism, as well as semantic differences between Sharia law and the Constitution. At this point, it must be noted that a growing pro-Muslim narrative was being cultivated within the White House when President Obama took office.

President George Bush, following September 11th, adopted not only the *war on terror* narrative but also a policy of appeasement toward Muslim communities within America. He intended to thwart any racial backlash following the terrorist attack by Islamists on American soil. To accomplish such, the President took a very pro-American Muslim position following the 9-11 attack, which included putting the leaders of Muslim organizations into the limelight. Additionally, the Muslim communities and agencies became proactive by giving blood and attending national memorials and Christian events to show their support.

On September 14, 2001, three days after the attacks, a National Day of Prayer and Remembrance ceremony was held at the National Cathedral in Washington, D.C. This memorial service, attended by the President, emphasized healing and unity. It was televised and hosted by numerous Washington diplomats, including members of Congress. An opening prayer was given by Dr. Muzammil H. Siddiqi, president of the Indiana-based Islamic Society of North America (ISNA). He was the first to read the Qur'an in a National Day of Prayer service. Other leaders representing Islamic institutions, such as Leaders of the American Muslim Political Coordination Council (AMPCC), Council on American-Islamic Relations (CAIR), and the Muslim Brotherhood (MB), were present to give condolences. In fact, on the very afternoon of 9-11, the President had scheduled a meeting with the AMPCC and a coalition of American-Muslim leaders to discuss a new Middle East Peace initiative.

American backlash was immediate and severe. There were attacks on Muslims and Islamic institutions throughout the country. President Bush publicly heightened his support for Muslim communities to counteract further American hostility. On September 17, he visited a Mosque and held an hour-long meeting at Washington D.C.'s Islamic Center. The meeting surveyed many topics, including "the need for American Muslim input on government policy."[169]

Subsequently, the President gave a press conference where he was given a "copy of the Qur'an and Paul Findley's book, *Silent No More: Confronting America's False Images of Islam.*" Notably, Paul Findley was a Republican with a strong propensity toward the Palestinian plight and forging communications with the Palestine Liberation Organization.[170]

On September 20th, President Bush addressed a joint session of Congress. He condemned the violence against Muslims as un-American and shameful in his speeches. He reframed the Islamic narrative: "Osama Bin Laden and his cohorts had "hijacked" Islam itself"—the otherwise peaceful religion. The effect was immediate. Violence and hate crimes dropped 95% that same day.

On September 26th, President Bush held another meeting with Muslim leaders, inviting those who had been stranded overseas due to the attacks. In this session, he etched in stone the new narrative the White House was going to adopt toward Islam: "Islam and their religion stand for 'goodness and peace.'" Unfortunately, the President's position was doing irrevocable damage to the American Muslims. By not distinguishing between moderate Muslims and Islamists, President Bush was encouraging, even facilitating, stealth jihad (discussed in chapter eight).

The distinction between American Muslims and Islamists is stark. American Muslims are, at most, traditional in their religious practice, American in their political aspirations, and secular in their daily lifestyles, while practicing Islamists are Muslims that adhere to Sharia law in their personal and community lives. They believe that Sharia law should be the ultimate Law of the land. They also support Islamic charities, education, and foreign entities affiliated with terrorist organizations.

With this narrative in place, President Obama was positioned to begin redefining America's domestic and global worldview towards Islam, thus opening the door for Sharia law to infiltrate into the fabric of American society rapidly.

Let's see exactly how the President and Islam undermined America through Stealth Jihad.

"The secret things belong unto the LORD our God: but those things which are revealed belong unto us and to our children forever, that we may do all the word of this law."

Deuteronomy 29:29

୫

CHAPTER EIGHT

Stealth Jihad

"Do you know Abner the son of Ner, that he came to deceive you, and to know your going out and your coming in, and to know all that you do." 2 Samuel 3:25

ဆာ

Now that we have looked at Sharia law and the emergence of *Takaful* since Obamacare let's turn our attention to the method Islamists are using to gain dominance in America through Sharia law: stealth jihad.

"Stealth what?" you might ask. Stealth is a word more familiar to you than you think. It's a cool way of saying "secret" or "hidden." It's like the word Trojan. You say Trojan, and anyone who knows Greek history thinks of the Trojan horse built as a gift for a king; and when the horse was delivered to the city gates of the king—surprise! An army jumped out and overtook the city. That is some serious betrayal and deception going on—a gift in the one hand and the sword in the other.

Stealth jihad is the same concept. It is infiltration or takeover of a nation through hidden, secret, and subversive agendas. "Stealth" is defined as "secret, hidden," while "jihad," in its most basic sense, means "struggle." In Islamic law, jihad is "the struggle against the infidels (the unbelievers) and the struggle to rule the world through the institution of Islamic law."[171] And that struggle can take on covert and overt manifestations. The overt expressions are what we see and read about in the daily news: terrorism and open incitement against Israel, as seen in the BDS Movement (Boycott, Divestment, and Sanctions). The covert manifestations are not readily detectable, but they surface first and foremost in money trails. Then they also show up in lawsuits, judicial compromise, the appearance of Mosques and cluster Islamic communities, and NGO organizations that fund anti-Israel agendas and terrorism. Most importantly, there is the infiltration of Islamic-centered individuals and organizations into critical political positions.

And no matter how American a Muslim is, if he adheres strictly to Islamic law, he cannot remain neutral about democracy and the United States Constitution, as they are an affront to Islam. Therefore, they will directly or indirectly aid in its overthrow. Time is not of the essence, only the goal. And the goal for every devout Islamist is to strategically move the chessboard pieces until they put the American government in checkmate.

∿

A New Narrative

Language does matter when drawing clear lines between good and evil, i.e., terrorism. With that said, the Obama administration not only continued the Bush narrative of Muslim goodwill, but it took it one step further by removing language that may be offensive to Muslims and dropping Bush's 'war on terror along with all narratives that associated Muslims with terrorism.

In 2011, Deputy Attorney General James Cole confirmed that the Obama administration was "pulling back all training materials used for law enforcement and national security communities, to eliminate all references to Islam."[172] This decision came after a 2009 indictment of 5 Muslims in the *Holy Land Foundation* terrorist finance trial. The trial did more than disclose the funneling of $12 million to Hamas; it also revealed the government's diverse views of Islam, terrorism, and Muslims. Upon hearing the Muslim references in the training manuals, there was an outcry from CAIR and other Muslim Brotherhood front groups, even though all these groups identified as having connections to Hamas in the trial.

This marked yet another phase of escalating Muslim advocacy over the Islamic narrative. Salam al-Marayati, President of the Muslim Public Affairs Council (MPAC), threatened the FBI in a Los Angeles Times op-ed.

He demanded that all "bigoted and inflammatory views" on Muslims be removed from all law enforcement training manuals. His Op-Ed cites a few examples such as, "'devout' Muslims are more prone toward violence, Islam 'aims to transform a country's culture into 7th-century Arabian ways', the Islamic charitable giving is a 'funding mechanism of combat,' and Mohammed was a "violent cult leader."[173] It also called for the Justice Department and the FBI to apologize and establish an 'interagency task force' to review training material and select trainers.

Furthermore, in his Op-Ed, Marayati cited a 2010 presentation by an analyst working for a U.S. attorney's office in Pennsylvania:

> 'Civilization Jihad' stretches back from the dawn of Islam and is waged today in the U.S. by 'civilians, juries, lawyers, media, academia, and charities who threaten 'our values.' The goal of that war: 'Replacement of American Judeo-Christian and Western liberal social, political, and religious foundations of Islam.[174]

This baseless statement, per Marayati, is at the heart of the goal of Islamic law, according to Maududi. What and whom Marayati cites is critical in understanding the depth of what he is attacking. It was far more than training material or inflammatory words. It was American values and ideology.

Salam Marayati was not without warrant in his Op-Ed, as he also attributes the Muslim community and its cooperation with law enforcement to thwarting at least 40% of terrorist attacks in America. On the other hand, the Op-Ed's tone, threats, and calculated inclusions earmarked a more serious development—intimidation works within the White House.

The Obama administration's response to Marayati and other Muslim advocacy groups' demands was irrational—a sign of government capitulation. It can be summed up with the statement of Dwight Holton, the U.S. Attorney in Oregon:

> I want to be perfectly clear about this: training materials that portray Islam as a religion of violence or with a tendency towards violence are wrong, they are offensive, and they are contrary to everything that this President, this Attorney General, and the Department of Justice stands for, and they will not be tolerated. The training materials pose a significant threat to National Security because they play into a false narrative propagated by terrorists that the United States is at war with Islam.[175]

This political move to change the training manuals was the beginning of the end of America's fight against Islam. It escalated the anti-Islam terrorist narrative and even led to a purge of Pentagon documents that mentioned Islam. Furthermore, terrorism on American soil was reduced to hate crimes.

⅋

Hate Crimes or Terrorism?

One of the most noticeable outcomes of the Obama administration's push to remove the term "Islam" from its association with terrorism or anti-American policy is the government's response to terrorist attacks on American soil. Between 2008 and 2016, there were a minimum of fourteen known terrorist attacks in America, resulting in 94 deaths and 368 wounded. In addition to terrorist attacks, seven recorded Sharia law honor killings resulted in 13 deaths.[176] In every instance, the appropriate narrative for a terrorist attack or honor killing was reduced to that of an individual psychopath and hate crime.

According to the Hate Crime Data Collection Guidelines, a Hate Crime is defined as "A criminal offense committed against a person or property which is motivated, in whole or in part, by the offender's bias against a race, religion, disability, sexual orientation, or ethnicity, national origin; also known as a Hate Crime."[177]

Terrorism, on the other hand, is defined by the FBI as "a federal crime of terrorism; an offense that is calculated to influence or affect the conduct of a government by intimidation or coercion." It also means to "retaliate against government conduct; and is a violation of one of the several listed statutes, including § 930(c) (relating to killing or attempted killing during an attack on a federal facility with a dangerous weapon); and § 1114 (relating to killing or attempted killing of officers and employees of the U.S.)."[178]

In addition to this broad definition of terrorism, the FBI has attributed three characteristics to "domestic terrorism:"

- Acts dangerous to human life that violates federal or state law;

- Acts intended (i) to intimidate or coerce a civilian population; (ii) to influence the policy of a government by intimidation or coercion; or (iii) to affect the conduct of a government by mass destruction, assassination, or kidnapping; and,

- Acts that occur primarily within the territorial jurisdiction of the United States.

This aversion to telling the truth and misleading the American people did not go unnoticed. Of late, former U.S. Representative Michelle Bachman remarked, "The Obama administration and its surrogates constantly act as the chief defenders of Islam, falling all over themselves to protect it from criticism after each new jihadist attack on America and Europe."

This comment falls upon the most recent outrage from a community in Idaho where a 5-year-old special needs girl was allegedly covered in urine, raped, and made to drink urine. The perpetrators were teenage and younger refugees from Sudan and Iraq. The government initially tried to cover up this incident. Subsequently, following its leak, Idaho General Attorney Wendy Olson gave a statement that set off a legal uproar over the First Amendment:

> "The spread of false information or inflammatory or threatening statements about the perpetrators or the crime itself reduces public safety and may violate federal law."[179]

In response to her statement, First Amendment attorney David Yerushalmi said,

"Ms. Olson's not-so-veiled threat is closer to an illegal speech by a government official than the speech she threatens, but this abuse of government power is no surprise coming from the political hacks this president has appointed in the U.S. attorney's office."

Irony has its place in every facet of life. And the Obama administration was full of it. It's ironic how the more it preached that Islam is a peaceful, just, and compassionate religion, the more angry, unjust, and non-compassionate the Obama administration became toward its American citizens.

In 2010, a compelling case sparked debate regarding Sharia law. Judge Joseph Charles, a New Jersey family court judge, refused to grant a restraining order to a woman being sexually abused by her Muslim Moroccan husband. The judge ruled that the man was behaving according to his Muslim beliefs. And in the Islamic religion, a woman should submit entirely to her husband's will, including abusive sexual relations. This decision was overruled by the Appellate Court of New Jersey, which held that the husband's religious beliefs were irrelevant to the case and that assault was illegal.[180]

In Oklahoma, the citizens introduced an amendment to the Constitution of Oklahoma, State Question 755, that stated, "The courts shall not look to the legal precepts of other nations or cultures. Specifically, the courts shall not consider international law or Sharia law."[181] This amendment, passed with 70% approval by the electorate in November 2010, was blocked by U.S. District Judge Vicki Miles-LaGrange. Her ruling was subsequently upheld by the Federal 10th Circuit Court of Appeals in Denver on January 10, 2012.

This case is interesting because the Federal Court blocked it for using the words "Sharia law" twice. Judge LaGrange argued that "singling out Sharia law conveys a message of disapproval of the Muslim faith, and has the effect of inhibiting the Muslim religion."[182]

This attempt to block an overwhelmingly approved Amendment because it inserted Sharia law two times indicates the influence Muslim organizations had within the Obama administration and the Judicial branch. The Constitution does not give the Judiciary branch of government the right to block or veto an amendment made by the people. Silencing the voice of Americans and their guaranteed rights of the First Amendment is being called into question at the highest Judicial level in American courts.

Michael Curtis further elaborates on the liberties of different religions and cultures within the United States. Rabbinical courts can function within Jewish communities, and America Indian tribal courts are fully functional. The difference is that these tribunals have not "intruded into the general legal system."[183] But, as noted in the abuse case tried by Judge Charles in New Jersey, Sharia law is attempting to intrude into the American judicial system.

Undoubtedly, Sharia law is not compatible with Constitutional law. And under the Obama administration, the U.S. government's protection of Sharia and its political correctness over its connection to Islam has brought into question the long-standing role of America as a leader in democratic freedoms and its Constitution as the Supreme Law of the land.

While writing this chapter, President Obama nominated the first Sharia-compliant Muslim federal judge, Abid Qureshi. He is a Pakistani immigrant who has practiced law in the United States for ten years and was educated at American universities. He has no judicial experience, but he does have "ties to Islamists, which include the Saudi Arabian government."

About Qureshi, editor Leo Hohmann writes,[184] "Most troubling for those concerned that Qureshi's allegiance to Islamic law may influence his view of the U.S. Constitution is his work representing a private school with ties to the hardline Saudi Arabian government in a case before the National Labor Relations Board."

Daniel Akbar, a former Sharia lawyer and Islamic expert for the Supreme Court of Iran, also weighed in on President Obama's nomination of Abid Qureshi:

An Islamist has an orthodox understanding of Islam. CAIR and ISNA have an orthodox understanding of the authoritative Islamic sources. If you have that, then you believe orthodox rules must rule a person's life. . ..If you are pro-even one law of Sharia, you are an Islamist. If you are someone coming from the Middle East and say, 'I don't give a damn about Muhammad and about Islam, but I'm a Muslim,' then you are not a problem. But if you are talking about someone with an orthodox understanding of Islam, then we should have a problem with you being a judge. So, we don't know if Mr. Qureshi is an Islamist or just a Muslim. But since I'm seeing on Twitter that CAIR and ISNA and all those activists for Sharia are supporting him, I'm suspicious he is an Islamist.[185]

The nomination of Qureshi expired on January 3, 2017, with the 114th Congress. Although he did not replace the seat vacated by Judge Rosemary M. Collyer, his nomination set a precedence for future nominations.

Such precedence mandates answers to underlying questions such as, is the candidate an Islamist? Can they objectively interpret the U.S. Constitution? If the White House frowns upon anti-Muslim rhetoric or the word Islamist cannot be used or recorded, how would the U.S. Senate question a candidate like Mr. Abid Qureshi? Would the Senate be able to inquire about the candidate's connections to Islamist organizations? And could they extrapolate vital information regarding the candidate's views on Sharia law without pushback from Muslim groups?

Because the Senate did not interview Mr. Qureshi, these questions still need to be asked and answered by future Muslim judicial candidates. How they play out remains to be seen.

૪૭

Stealth Jihad

The escalating government threats regarding anti-Muslim rhetoric are a direct infringement upon the First

Amendment of the Constitution, "Congress shall not abridge 'the freedom of speech.'" Unfortunately, Congress did not have the opportunity to weigh in on the Islamic-Muslim conundrum. During his tenure, President Obama bypassed the legislative branch and dictated to the Judicial, Military, and National Security arms of government rhetoric, norms, and laws surrounding Islamic terrorism, Muslim immigration, Muslim refugees, anti-Muslim rhetoric, and Sharia law.

Now. let's turn our attention to observations on how American democracy is perceived by Islam and subverted through stealth jihad. Such an overview enumerates how and why the Obama administration failed to create a narrative that accurately reflected Islamic Sharia law: a very present threat to the future of Democracy and Constitutional supremacy in the United States of America.

Sadly, throughout the Obama presidency, the demands and threats of the Muslim lobby influenced an intentional narrative from the White House to create an illusion of peace surrounding Islam as a religion. From the onset, Obama placed members of the Muslim Brotherhood into key staff positions. These staff members played a significant role in fashioning Obama's anti-Islamic worldview and the legal framework used to persuade Justices to block or violate American Constitutional freedoms, as presented in the Oklahoma amendment case.

Such actions on behalf of the former President can be understood as contributing to the erosion of Constitutional authority. There are also numerous other lobby capitulations and legal actions under the guise of "human rights" that one can point to, such as the legalization of same-sex marriage. Still, they are not within the scope of this chapter.

The objective of the Obama presidency was to ensure the protection of the American Muslim community and reshape the Islamic Muslim image from that of terrorists to one of peace and compatibility. It also intended to disenfranchise terrorism from its Islamic roots and Sharia law. This not only projected a false narrative regarding Islam, but it also failed to address the actual threat that America faces: an ideological threat crouched in stealth Jihad—an internal Jihad working to overthrow the Constitution of the United States of America as the supreme law of the land.

One of the most erroneous claims of Islam is that Sharia law is a religious law and, therefore, in the U.S., it is protected by the First Amendment of the Constitution. However, Sharia law is a "totalitarian socio-political doctrine" which places it outside the First Amendment. Sharia means "the path," and though it has a spiritual component such as prayer five times a day, it possesses a "comprehensive legal and political framework."[186] Patrick Poole, military and law enforcement consultant on anti-terrorism issues, and Joseph Schmitz, former Inspector General, Department of Defense, remarked, "it would be a mistake to think of Sharia as a "religious" code in the Western sense because it seeks to regulate all manner of behavior in the secular sphere—economic, social, military, legal and political."[187] As evidenced throughout portions of this book, Sharia law is making inroads into each of these channels of civilian life.

The divide and debate within Islam and among Muslims who practice Sharia appear to be among moderate Muslims who hold Sharia as a code of personal conduct and Muslims who see Sharia as supreme law. Those who see Sharia as supreme law are known as Muslim supremacists or Islamists. It is the latter category that the Obama presidency failed to identify, isolate, and abrogate from the democratic government of the United States.

Islamists purport a global totalitarian concept of conquest known as a caliphate. Sharia law is their religious-social-political system—a system all Muslims are mandated to uphold and all Westerners must submit to. The method for bringing about their objectives throughout the West is "stealth jihad." For Islamists, "stealth jihad" is a "civil, internal jihad often called 'dawa'—a call to Islam." It characteristically is marked by a non-violent means to infiltrate government and society.

Tactics utilized to employ "stealth Jihad" are found in the Qur'an under the guise of lying and deceit. Did you know that the Qur'an permits lying and deception to overthrow an enemy, i.e., American democracy? This tactic is known as Taqiyya. In addition, Islamists use other forms of deceit such as Kitman: Lying by omission, Tawriya: Intentionally creating a false impression, and Muruna: 'Blending in' by setting aside some practices of Islam or Sharia to advance others.

Here are just a few examples from the Hadith and Islamic Law[188]:

<u>Sahih Bukhari (52:269)</u> - "The Prophet said, 'War is deceit.'" The context of this is thought to be the murder of Usayr ibn Zarim and his thirty unarmed men by Muhammad's men after he "guaranteed" them safe passage.

<u>Sahih Bukhari (49:857)</u> - "He who makes peace between the people by inventing good information or saying good things, is not a liar." Lying is permitted when the end justifies the means.

Islamic Law: Reliance of the Traveler (p. 746 - 8.2) "Speaking is a means to achieve objectives. If a praiseworthy aim is attainable through both telling the truth and lying, it is unlawful to accomplish it with lying because there is no need for it. When it is possible to achieve such an aim by lying but not by telling the truth, it is permissible to lie if attaining the goal is permissible (i.e., when the purpose of lying is to circumvent someone who is preventing one from doing something permissible), and obligatory to lie if the goal is obligatory. . ..it is religiously precautionary in all cases to employ words that give a misleading impression. . .."

As the intent of "stealth jihad" is to "sabotage" a nation from within, it often camouflages itself in "moderation." Islamists take on the role of "moderate" Muslims who enjoin themselves in Sharia-based organizations and subsequently present themselves as "moderates and servants" when negotiating differences within society. Yet, their community and home life are explicitly governed by Sharia law—Linda Sansour[189] is an excellent example. And since Sharia is a totalitarian system—it is imputed upon all aspects of civil society and human life, both public and private.

Regardless of how it is cloaked or uncloaked, Sharia law is anti-Constitutional. No rhetoric, dialogue, or government inclusion can change the Sharia discourse. Why? Because Sharia fundamentally rejects democratic tenets, which are the bedrock of American society and values. It outright rejects the rights of the governed to "'make law for themselves; freedom of conscience as displayed through self-government and individual liberty; freedom of expression which includes the right to criticize sharia; economic liberty which includes the right to private property; equitable treatment for both male and female; freedom from cruel and harsh punishment, inclusive of the use of terrorism; and the use of 'mechanisms of federalism and democracy' to resolve political differences."[190]

The realization that there are Muslim organizations within America that seek to supplant the American Constitution through "stealth jihad" or "civilization jihad" should not be ignored.

During the United States vs. Holy Land Foundation terrorist finance trial in 2008, the *Explanatory Memorandum on the General Strategic Goal for the Group*[191] was entered as evidence. The document was written in 1991 by Mohamed Akram, a senior Hamas leader in the U.S. and a member of the

Board of Directors of the Muslim Brotherhood (MB) in North America. The MB is also known as the Ikhwan.

Understanding the term Ikhwan is essential because the document clarifies that the Islamic Movement is "a Muslim Brotherhood effort, led by the Ikhwan in America."

Who are Ikhwan's? Muslim Brotherhood ideologues such as Abu al-A'la Maududi, Hassan al-Banna, and Sayyid Qutb. They are known as "Ikhwan ideologues." They are those who have "recast modern jihad in the fiery language of revolution and anti-colonialism. . .. and not just strictly warfare to expand Islamic legal and political dominance."[192] All three have adopted a narrative that declares *the overthrow of unjust governments to be lawful.*[193]

Furthermore, Qutb, in his book *Milestones*, refers to the abolishment of all "satanic forces and satanic systems of life" as a reason for Jihad. According to Team B II, "satanic systems of life" means "the way of life practiced in western-style liberal democracies—the way of the infidel, the Westerner, the non-Muslim."[194] Hence, Ikhwans are those enjoined to the Muslim Brotherhood who follow, practice, and execute the ideology of these three Ikhwan idealogues.[195]

A closer look at the Explanatory Memorandum reveals its stealth jihad agenda:

Paragraph 1, §§1 and 2, Explanatory Memorandum, 18, reads:

The general strategic goal of the Group in America, which was approved by the Shura Council and the Organizational

Conference for the year [1987] is "Enablement of Islam in North America, meaning: establishing an effective and stable Islamic Movement led by the Muslim Brotherhood which adopts Muslim' causes domestically and globally, and which works to expand the observant Muslim base, aims at unifying and directing Muslims' efforts, presents Islam as a civilization alternative, and supports the global Islamic State wherever it is."

Paragraph 4 of the Explanatory Memorandum, 20, describes the "Process of Settlement":

In order for Islam and its Movement to become "a part of the homeland" in which it lives, "stable" in its land, "rooted" in the spirits and minds of its people, and "enabled" in the lives of its society and has firmly-established "organizations" on which the Islamic structure is built and with which the testimony of civilization is achieved, the Movement must plan and struggle to obtain, "the keys" and "the tools" of this process in carrying out this grand mission as a "Civilization Jihadist" responsibility which lies on the shoulders of Muslims and—on top of them—the Muslim Brotherhood in this country. Among these keys and tools are the following. ."

Lastly, Paragraph 4, §4, of the Explanatory Memorandum refers to "Understanding the role of the Muslim Brotherhood in North America." It reads as follows:

The Process of settlement is a "Civilization-Jihadist Process" with all the word means. The Ikhwan must understand that their work in America is a kind of grand Jihad in eliminating and destroying Western Civilization from within and "sabotaging" its miserable house by their hands and the hands of believers so that it is eliminated and God's religion is made victorious over all other religions. . ..It is a Muslim's destiny to perform Jihad and work wherever he is and wherever he lands until the final hour comes, and there is no escape from that destiny except for those who chose to slack."

This "Explanatory Memorandum" reflects Hamas' Charter Article 2:[196]

The Islamic Resistance Movement is the branch of the Muslim Brotherhood in Palestine. The Muslim Brotherhood is a global organization and the most prominent Islamic movement in modern times. It excels in profound understanding and has an exact, fully comprehensive perception of all Islamic concepts in all areas of life: understanding and thought, politics and economics, education and social affairs, law and government, spreading (i.e., indoctrinating the tenets of radical) Islam and teaching, art and the media, by that which is hidden and by martyrdom and in the other areas of life.

Article 6 of the Hamas Charter opens another caveat in the Obama administration: The progressive distancing itself from Israel.

The Islamic Resistance Movement is uniquely Palestinian. It has faith in Allah and adopts Islam as its way of life. It acts to fly the banner of Allah over all of Palestine because people of all religions can live in the shadow of Islam in tranquility and security for their lives, property, and rights. However, in the absence of Islam, a conflict develops that injustice, corruption grows, more conflicts are created, and [eventually] war breaks out.

Although Jihad, external or internal, is present within the Muslim Brotherhood, it too was excised from the Obama Muslim doctrine and removed from its terrorist list. John Brennan, Obama's top counterterrorism advisor, insisted that President [Obama] did not believe there was a "global war" with Islamic terrorists. And because of such, Brennan announced that "the term 'jihadists' will no longer be used to describe our enemies."[197] He reserved using the term to describe al Qaeda's ruthless operatives. This lack of understanding of the goal and connection of jihad to Sharia law and Islam's obligation to sabotage American democracy for the greater moral good revealed two things: the effectiveness of the lobby of Islamic organizations[198] and the ease with which "stealth jihad" operated within the Obama administration.

For America, the question remains: How valuable are democracy and its freedoms? Is it worth fighting for? Suppose the agenda of Islamists indeed is to deceive America through stealth jihad. How can their plan be exposed without infringing the rights or inflicting harm on moderate American Muslims?

How could the trend of Islamic appeasement be reversed within the Trump administration? And would it be in the best interest of democracy to call out "stealth jihad" and insist that the Islamists remove all anti-American rhetoric, process of settlement, civilization Jihad, grand Jihad, stealth Jihad strategy, indoctrination of radical tenets, terrorism support, sedition, and inclination to subvert the Constitution from their charters, training manuals, and organizational documents? With a new President, maybe it is time to restore American Democracy and the supremacy of its law and the Constitution so that all people can have the right to liberty, freedom, and the pursuit of happiness.

৪৩

The List

Following is a list of organizations associated with the Muslim Brotherhood:[199]

- Islamic Society of North America (ISNA)
- Muslim Student Association (MSA)
- Muslim Communities Association (MCA)
- Association of Muslim Social Scientists (AMSS)
- Association of Muslim Scientists and Engineers (AMSE)
- Islamic Medical Association (IMA)
- Islamic Teaching Center (ITC)
- North American Islamic Trust (NAIT)
- Foundation for International Development (FID)
- Islamic Housing Cooperative (IHC)
- Islamic Centers Division (ICD)
- American Trust Publications (ATP)
- Audio-Visual Center (AVC)
- Islamic Book Service (IBS)
- Muslim Businessmen Association (MBA)
- Muslim Youth of North America (MYNA)
- ISNA Fiqh Committee (IFC)
- ISNA Political Awareness Committee (IPAC)
- Islamic Education Department (IED)

- Muslim Arab Youth Association (MAYA)

- Malaysian (sic) Islamic Study Group (MISG)

- Islamic Association for Palestine (IAP)

- United Association for Studies and Research (UASR)

- Occupied Land Fund (OLF)

- Mercy International Association (MIA)

- Islamic Circle of North America (ICNA)

- Baitul Mal Inc (BMI)

- International Institute for Islamic Thought (IIIT)

- Islamic Information Center (IIC)

Several of the preeminent Muslim-American organizations in the United States today (notably, the Council on American-Islamic Relations [CAIR], the Muslim Public Affairs Council [MPAC], and the Islamic Free Market Institute [II]) were not established in 1991 when the Muslim Brotherhood adopted this document.

To be considered by the Muslim Brotherhood to be one of "our organizations" or an "organization of our friends," each of these entities had to embrace the Ikhwan creed: "Allah is our goal; the Messenger is our guide: the Qur'an is our law; Jihad is our means, and martyrdom in the way of Allah is our inspiration."

"When your country cherishes life, you'll do everything possible to save one."

Magen David Adom

ෂ

CHAPTER NINE

Betraying Israel

". . .there will I deal with and execute judgment upon them for the treatment of My people and My heritage Israel, whom they have scattered among the nations and because they have divided My land." Joel 3:2

ഔ

On September 20th, 2016, President Obama addressed the United Nations, General Assembly. In his farewell address, he sidelined America's loyalty to the nation of Israel by stating that "Israel must recognize that it cannot 'permanently occupy Palestinian land.'" Rhetoric for underscoring the validity of a two-state solution. Obama added that the Palestinians must also "reject incitement and recognize Israel's legitimacy."

Here we have the peanut butter sandwich of demands: recognize, reject, recognize. Even though, at face value, these requests seem reasonable, when taken apart, there is a considerable gap in the Truth O Meter between the two.

First, the Palestinians are a non-state actor. They are not a nation, a legitimate state, or a recognized partner for peace. World leaders want to legitimize them, but thus far, the Palestinians have rejected all proposals and Israel's right to exist—for this reason, they don't have a state—even the EU desperately wants to pretend they do. Oddly, you will find on Wikipedia the following about Mahmoud Abbas,

> Mahmoud Abbas, also known by the kunya Abu Mazen, is the president of the State of Palestine and the Palestinian National Authority. He has been the chairman of the Palestine Liberation Organization since 11 November 2004, PNA president since 15 January 2005, and State of Palestine president since 8 May 2005.[200]

Wikipedia falsely states that Abbas is the president of a State that does not exist. And he has been the president since 2005, the year of the Disengagement of Gush Katif. Israel may have sacrificed Gush Katif, but it never finalized a two-state solution. The Palestinians have yet to agree on any terms for an independent state.

Hence, the European Union, United Nations, Obama, and most recently, the Biden dream team have created a fictitious reality ignoring the facts—the Palestinians are occupying Israel's land, not the other way around. On the flip side, Israel doesn't see the Palestinians as occupiers or as a State. They are welcome under Israel's sovereignty—unless they commit acts of terrorism.

With that said, I would like to share an insight rarely mentioned regarding the two-state solution—the choice of the Palestinian people.

As we discussed in the last two chapters, the Muslim Brotherhood has an agenda to replace the U.S. Constitution with Sharia Law or, at the very least, use the Constitution to impose Sharia Law upon the American Muslim society. For many democratically inclined Muslims, that is a horrifying thought. And for most Palestinians living under the democratic rule of Israel, it is equally frightening.

During my discussions with young Palestinian women, they unanimously told me that they do not want to be under the control of Hamas, the militant wing of the Muslim Brotherhood, Abbas and the PLO, or any Sharia-based government. They would prefer to remain under the autonomy of Israel. For many young Palestinians, the whole Islam initiative is a real turn-off. They don't want to be forced to pray, yet they want to pray. Nor do they want to be compelled to wear burqas, niqabs, or hijabs. Instead, they desire to choose their religious involvement, integrate into Israeli society, attend college, become professionals, have careers, start families and live the semblance of more democratic and free life.

For this reason, alone, we must find another solution than the old, out-of-date, and unwanted two-state solution. Putting the Palestinian people under the bondage and oppression of Sharia Law by agreeing to a two-state solution—is not upholding human rights, a just Middle East democracy, or religious freedom.

Of course, there is also the issue of the West Bank, the biblical land of Judea and Samaria—Israeli territory that the European Union and United Nations want to give to the Palestinian Authority. Strategically, this makes the two-state solution a death trap for Israel. Let me explain why:

First, towards the end of the Obama era, the Palestinian Authority (PA) was losing political ground, and the resignation of President Mahmoud Abbas was looming.[201] The implications of such could increase the influence of Hamas, the terrorist organization that controls Gaza —begging the question, "if the West Bank is given over to the Palestinians and the PA disbanded, would it naturally fall into the hands of Hamas and the Al-Quds Brigades?"

Since President Trump took office, a concerted effort began within his administration to bring peace to the Middle East.

Abbas did a 180. He came out of the shadows of near retirement to lead in the peace negotiations. He was tasked with reigning in Hamas and creating a unity government. To accomplish a reconciliatory vision, Abbas put the squeeze on Gaza—reducing both electric and water supply rations due to bills that were in arrears. His tactic was intended to: 1) cause Hamas to surrender control over Gaza and 2) demonize Israel by making it appear that Israel was callously withholding aid to Gaza.

On November 1, 2017, Hamas handed over five border crossings to the Palestinian Authority (PA), also known as Fatah. The handover, brokered by Egypt, was part of a signed agreement to restore the status quo in Gaza after the 2007 split between the PA and Hamas. It is believed that this initial step, with more to come, will result in a better quality of life for the Gazan citizens.[202]

As beautiful as it appears on the surface, a unity government between Hamas and the PA conjures up deep concerns as to the ultimate end game for Mahmoud Abbas. Mahmoud Abbas is a "foreign leader who harbors or supports terrorism."[203] Yes, he controls the Al Aqsa Martyrs' Brigade[204], a division of Fatah and a terrorist organization on the U.S terror list. And, if you ponder that Abbas was grooming a terrorist in prison to replace him, then it is easy to see that the absence of a Hamas-controlled Gaza does not equate to no terror. On the contrary, Hamas continues aligning with Iran and its growing regional axis. And, as a show of spite towards the U.S., just days before Abbas met President Trump at the White House, the Al Aqsa Martyrs' Brigade staged a public rally in full regalia, firing weapons. Furthermore, the PA continues to fund terrorists and their family members. And if this is the reality of what is touted as a "partner for peace" without state status, what do you think will unfold if Abbas and the PA negotiated state status?

In addition to the PA conundrum, to consider the challenges to Israel's National Security, we must look at the whole picture: Hamas in Gaza, the Al Aqsa Martyrs' Brigade spread out in Palestinian communities, the terrorist group Al-Quds in the West Bank, Hezbollah is Iran's proxy parked along the Lebanese border and now in the Lebanese government, and Iran is building a land bridge from Tehran to Beirut, while ISIS gathers along the Egyptian border. Under a two-state solution, this scenario would be heightened tenfold. And with the Obama-infused funds of the U.S. government,[205] Iran's funding of terrorist organizations such as Hamas, Hezbollah, and Islamic Jihad[206] has never been more volatile.

On August 15th, Deborah Danan wrote an excellent article for Breitbart entitled *Hezbollah, Hamas Officials Confirm Iran Funds Our Activity*. She quotes Nasrallah, the Secretary General of Hezbollah, while speaking to Lebanon's Al Ahed news (translated by the Middle East Media Research Institute (MEMRI). He clarified Hezbollah's budget source:

> Hezbollah's budget—its salaries and expenditures, food and drink, weapons and missiles—[all come from] Iran. Is that clear?… As long as Iran has money, we have money. Do you require greater transparency than that[?] The funds earmarked for us do not reach us through the banks. We receive them the same way we receive our missiles with which we threaten Israel.

Her article further captures Iran's funding of Hamas. Abu Marzouq, deputy head of Hamas's political bureau, tweeted on June 15, "The aid extended by Iran to the Palestinian resistance in provisions, training, and funds are not comparable [to any other aid], and most other countries cannot match it." Also, former Lebanese minister and known supporter of Hezbollah

Wiam Wahhab tweeted, "Iran funded resistance in Palestine to restore Jerusalem, Al-Aqsa, and the Church of the Sepulcher." Note that the funding is not to build an infrastructure for the Palestinian people but terrorism.

Lastly, I would like to mention the terrorist group Palestinian Islamic Jihad (PIJ), whose militant wing is called Al-Quds Brigades.[207] This organization operates out of the West Bank, with its strongholds located primarily in Hebron and Jenin.[208] Along with Hamas, Al-Quds formed as an offshoot of the Muslim Brotherhood. And they, too, are funded by Iran. Danan writes:

> Iran also restored aid to the Gaza-based Islamic Jihad after suspending its support to the terror group following disagreements concerning the crisis in Yemen. *Al-Sharq Al-Awsat* reported that an Islamic Jihad delegation headed by secretary-general Ramadan Shalah visited Iran in April 2016; during this visit, Tehran renewed its sponsorship of the organization after the latter accepted its terms.

The above is just a taste of numerous articles and speeches that cite Iran's involvement in supporting terrorism against Israel. But the real issue is that these terrorist organizations have only one agenda—to delegitimize Israel and wipe Israel off the map. For this reason, it would be foolish to reward terrorists with a state. Hence, supporting a two-state solution is rewarding terrorism and sanctioning their anti-Israel agenda.

☙

Gush Katif

Do you remember Gush Katif? A beautiful, cultivated bloc of seventeen Jewish communities located in Southern Gaza. These communities were the buffer zone between Egypt and Gaza. It was the summer of 2005 when the IDF forcibly removed the remaining citizens of these communities from their homes. Ten thousand plus Israeli citizens turned over their homes, businesses, educational facilities, and operational plants to the Palestinian Authority as a gesture of peace, only to watch them destroyed. What did Israel get in return? A Hamas terrorist base and training camp that, in 2014, launched over 4,000 missiles into Israel.

Gush Katif was a futile exercise in self-delusion among World leaders, a callisthenic in appeasement led by the United States State Department.[209] One terrorist base and training camp are more than enough. To turn a blind eye to the reality that Hamas would also turn the West Bank into a second terrorist base is to be an accomplice to mass murder and Israel's potential annihilation.

But, other solutions and opportunities, primarily through education, social media, women, and youth, produce steps towards a path to peace rather than a two-state solution.

The narrative purported by the United Nations and anti-Israel NGOs is making the world believe that Israel illegally occupies the West Bank. This dangerously deceptive lie leads us back to Obama's second statement during his final U.N. address.

The second statement Obama made was correct; Israel is a legitimate nation with borders. Israel's borders, which include the West Bank (Judea and ancient Shomron), were purchased with Israeli blood, sweat, and tears in 1967 after five Arab nations presumptuously attacked Israel with the intent to destroy her. In Sunday's Jerusalem Post (September 25, 2016), Oded Revivi wrote an excellent commentary entitled, *Mr. President: The Israeli settlements are legal*. Concerning the legality of 1967 borders, he said:

> The State of Israel captured territory that did not belong to any other country and was already designated for establishing the Jewish State. The legal status of Palestine, which the Balfour Declaration (1917) earmarked as the future "national home for the Jewish people," was determined by the League of Nations (1920), the San Remo agreements (1920), and the British Mandate, in addition to being approved by the US Congress (1922). In the absence of any other laws, these laws still apply today, making Israel's presence legal and valid.

Obama's narrative that Israel is a legitimate country that cannot permanently occupy the land of an illegitimate state is equivalent to calling evil good and good evil. Once again, we find President Obama on the side of illegal, misguiding Americans regarding its faithful ally Israel. Wherever you stand on the two-state solution, it's time for a new path to peace.

Saudi Arabia

Before we leave this chapter, let's talk about Saudi Arabia. Since the first meeting in Riyadh with the Trump Team (Jared Kushner and Jason Greenblatt) to further Middle East Peace between Israel, the Palestinians, and the Arab world, the Saudi government has stepped out of the shadows as a U.S. ally and mediator between the Israeli and Palestinian peace agreement.

The recent actions of the Saudi heir, Crown Prince Mohammed bin Salman is shaking both the ME region and Saudi Arabia itself! Reports of new laws allowing women to drive and the arrests of Saudi's political elites on corruption charges are flowing from Arab media outlets. And on behalf of the U.S., Saudi has forced the resignation of Lebanese Prime Minister Hariri and given an ultimatum to Palestinian Authority President Abbas—accept Trump's plan or resign in anticipation of a peace deal that would be agreed upon by Israel, the Palestinians, and even the Sunni Shia Muslim world.

However, the real highlight is Crown Prince Salman's *Saudi Arabia Vision 2030*.[210] In an interview with Al Arabiya TV, the Prince confirmed that an IPO[211] of approximately 5% of Aramco stock, Saudi's largest oil company, will be released. He also highlighted the following three pillars:

- The first pillar is our status as the heart of the Arab and Islamic worlds.
- The second pillar is our determination to become a global investment powerhouse.

- The third pillar is transforming our unique strategic location into a global hub connecting three continents, Asia, Europe, and Africa.

With *Vision 2030,* Saudi Arabia is poised to lead the Arab world toward westernization and modernization. What's interesting is that Ezekiel foresaw this 2500 years ago.[212]

The Obama administration has consistently refused to recognize Jerusalem as Israeli territory, let alone as the capital of Israel.

Ben Shapiro

୫୦

CHAPTER TEN

Foreign Policy

"You shall not pervert judgment; you shall not respect persons (or foreign leaders), neither take a gift: for a gift (bribe) does blind the eyes of the wise, and pervert the words of the righteous." Deuteronomy 16:19

ಹಿ

Have you seen the movie Thirteen Hours? It is the true story of the terrorist attack on the United States consulate and CIA outpost in Benghazi. It speaks volumes of the failed foreign policy of the Obama administration and the Clinton State Department. You cannot watch the movie and not wonder, "why?" Hearing the words, "I called for air cover, they never came," near the end of the movie leaves you numb and enraged over the intentional negligence of the United States Government. How could our government let this happen?

That same question followed us to Afghanistan. Few realize that U.S. soldiers were being killed in Afghanistan, not because of terrorism or sniper fire, but because our troops did not receive the clearance, weapons, or assets they needed to fight. This results from an administration that sells out the American ethos of "I pledge allegiance to my Flag and the Republic for which it stands, one nation under God, indivisible, with liberty and justice for all."

Let's just take a glimpse at what failed foreign policy looks like.

Hillary Clinton served as Secretary of State from 2009 - 2013. In just five years, she left a death toll estimated between 700,000 to 2 million in her wake.[213] The failed foreign policy under her watch resulted in Russian expansionism, China's Nine-Dash line, the rise and expansion of ISIL, the Syrian Refugee crimes and crisis, and Iran's terror trifecta.

To understand why, let's go back to 2008, just before President Obama and Secretary of State Clinton stepped on the scene.

While Obama campaigned on improving Russian relations in 2008, few realized what this meant for the Eastern Block of Europe—countries under Soviet control during the Cold War. When Russia invaded Georgia in 2008, the United States stepped in immediately by deploying U.S. warships to the Black Sea and recalling Georgia troops from Iraq. President Bush also froze bilateral relations with Russia. He then went one step further to protect the Eastern Block with plans to build installations that housed missile defense interceptors, which Poland and the Czech Republic agreed to host.

After Hillary was appointed Secretary of State, her first assignment was to follow through on Obama's vision for Russian revival. Hence, in March 2009, she met with Russian Foreign Minister Sergei Lavrov. Six months later, the U.S. canceled the deployment of the interceptors to Poland and the Czech Republic, leaving them without the economic or security benefits we promised.

Let's bring this down to a personal level. Have you ever been betrayed by a friend for personal gain? This often happens in high school when girlfriends steal boyfriends and vice versa. It also happens when opportunity knocks to climb the corporate ladder or when family members come into an inheritance. Amazing how quickly one can betray another when personal gain is involved. I am not saying you would—and hopefully, your character is better than that, but none of us are exempt from its temptation. Whether you have or haven't—our government has, and neither Poland nor the Czech Republic has forgotten.

Russia's Vladimir Putin, on the other hand, immediately perceived this buttering up to Russia and subsequent concessions for what it was—American betrayal. Notably, he had already given Poland and the Czech Republic a tongue lashing for siding with America. Now that they were humiliated by the World's Sovereign, Putin's expansionist agenda could move forward—Crimea, the Middle East, Georgia, and Ukraine. With the only superpower holding

Russia in check bought with a bribe, who would now keep Russia in check?

In his article, Hillary Clinton's Foreign Policy Failures, Jonathan Levin writes that this was "the first of what would become a pattern, the U.S. sacrificed allies' interests to a rival in the fatuous hope that the rival would feel some sort of gratitude or obligation in return." Has that happened? Does Russia feel a "sort of gratitude" or obligation to America and her interest? I say not, considering that Ukraine is fighting for its existence, a war against Russia that the U.S. had no leverage to stop—but most certainly could have prevented.

On the night of the third debate between Trump and Clinton, I was sitting in a hospital family lounge waiting to return to a dear friend's room. The TV was on, and I just happened to catch the Clinton-Trump exchange over the Russian hacks. From my perspective, Clinton attempted to make Trump a scapegoat for the hacked emails uploaded by WikiLeaks. She also pointed the finger at him for Russian espionage and being a close buddy of Vladimir Putin—like that was a horrible thing. My mouth opened, and the familiar words blurted out, "what a liar." You see, I had just finished researching documents on Clinton and Russia, which the above only scrapped the surface. You know that's what guilty people do; they transfer blame to the other.

On a side note, have you asked why Russia would hack Hillary, Podesta, Soros, the State Department, etc.? Well, not because of Trump, I assure you. Remember the Panama Paper Scandal in chapter one? There is your answer. This group went after Putin, and Russia was just returning the favor—giving them a little taste of their own medicine, wouldn't you say? Now back to Clinton and Trump.

Do you remember the cookie jar on the kitchen counter? The one your mother said, "don't touch?" Well, I loved the cookie jar growing up. I would sneak a few cookies and then cover up my naughty escapade by rearranging the cookies in the cookie jar, so it looked fuller. One day, my mother noticed almost all the cookies were gone and called all of us kids to the kitchen. She lined us up and asked, "who ate the cookies?" We all shook our heads "no." "No one ate the cookies?" mom asked, raising her voice. "Nope," we all muttered under our breaths. Finally, I spoke up and blamed my brother. "Yep," my brother did it. He got a spanking, and I felt horrible that he took the punishment for my cookie sins. I am unsure if I ever confessed, but I stopped making my brother the scapegoat for my hand in the cookie jar. The connection?

Trump was Hillary's scapegoat for her folly with Russia, and the media just played along.

Do you remember the Uranium One deal? It was another deal brokered in secret under the guise of the "Russian reset," giving Russia 20% of U.S. Uranium assets.

In May 2016, Peter Schweizer, author of Clinton Cash, wrote in his article, *One Year of Silence on Hillary Clinton's Uranium Deal*[214] the following:

A few days later, things got worse for the Clintons when two *New York Times* Pulitzer Prize-winning investigative reporters, Jo Becker and Mike McIntire, took two of the most explosive chapters in the book and did their own digging. What they found confirmed what I had reported. They ran a 3,000-word, front-page article in the paper confirming that: Bill and Hillary Clinton had helped a Canadian financier named Frank Giustra and a small Canadian company obtain a lucrative uranium mining concession from the dictator in Kazakhstan; The same Canadian company, renamed Uranium One, bought uranium concessions in the United States; The Russian government came calling and sought to buy that Canadian company for a price that would mean big profits for the Canadian investors; For the Russians to buy that Canadian company, it required the approval of the Obama administration, including Hillary's State Department, because uranium is a strategically important commodity; Nine shareholders in Uranium One just happened to provide more than $145 million in donations to the Clinton Foundation in the run-up to State Department approval; Some of the donations, including those from the Chairman of Uranium One, Ian Teler, were kept secret, even though the Clintons promised to disclose all donations; Hillary's State Department approved the deal; The Russian government now owns 20 percent of U.S. uranium assets.

In short, this was what you might call "a radioactive scandal." It included secret donations, the Russian government, foreign financiers, more than $145 million, and Bill and Hillary Clinton.

Concerning Clinton's bribery, *RealClearPolitics* wrote,

If foreign governments, including adversarial ones like Russia, paid the Clinton Foundation vast sums of money, they assured themselves favorable treatment. (Mr. Clinton received $500,000 for a Moscow speech from a Russian investment bank with links to the Kremlin that was pursuing the purchase of Uranium One, a uranium mining company.)[215]

And then there was the post-agreement interview with Rosatom's chief executive, Sergei Kiriyenko, who told Putin, "Few could have imagined in the past that we would own 20 percent of U.S. reserves."[216]

Rosatom is Russia's atomic energy corporation. It has regional centers in Western, Central, and Eastern Europe, Latin America, Central Asia, East, and South-East Asia, the Middle East, and North Africa.[217] The India Times reported the following:

According to South Asia CEO Alexey Pimenov, the worldwide creation of a regional center's network was due to the expansion of Rosatom's global presence and a long-term development strategy, according to which the purpose of the company for the next ten years was to increase the portfolio of foreign orders up to $150 billion. Recently, Rosatom opened a regional center in Mumbai, India.[218]

So, while the end of the Cold War was supposed to bring Nuclear Arms depreciation between the U.S. and Russia, and while the Obama administration was actively depreciating our U.S. Nuclear Arms capabilities to create a safer non-nuclear world, Russia was busy building its nuclear presence across the globe. Oh, and I don't want to forget that Iran is too! But then again, we should have expected such because Obama leads from behind. Yes, and all the while, the Clintons seemed to be at the top of the Hill in the nuclear business.

Lastly, when it comes to bribes, the kind of bribes that blind judgment, check this report out:

More than half, to be exact, at least 85 of 154 people from private interests who met or had phone conversations scheduled with Clinton while she led the State Department donated to her family charity or pledged commitments to its international programs, according to a review of State Department calendars released so far to The Associated Press. Combined, the 85 donors contributed as much as $156 million. At least 40 donated more than $100,000 each, and 20 gave more than $1 million.[219]

Those are staggering numbers that cannot be ignored. The question one must ask after reading the documented depth of bribery is, "what will America's future hold if the American people willingly ignore the truth?"

Let's move on to the Asian pivot—Russia's there too!

಄

Asian Pivot

The 2011 Asian shift is the "pivot" in American foreign policy. This pivot from the Middle East to Asia is called the "Potemkin pivot." Have you ever heard the word "Potemkin?" Well, here it is, a new Scrabble word.

Potemkin means "having a false or deceptive appearance, especially one presented for curating propaganda."[220] It also has the connotation of fraudulent or counterfeit. The term came from the surname of a Russian soldier named Grigori Aleksandrovich (1739-91). He was the lover of Empress Catherine II. To impress her into believing Crimea was a rich country, he built a fake village known as the Potemkin village along the banks of the Dnieper River. Hence, the "Potemkin pivot" in foreign policy exists "solely to impress."

Those who understand the Obama doctrine shift from the Middle East to Asia will quickly point out that Clinton was center stage in this shift; and that no propagandized message could redeem the domino effect of the destruction it triggered. Without question, the "pivot," which later became known as the "Rebalance of Asia," enhanced the U.S. presence in Asia—one that was severely lacking. The most notable outgrowth of America's presence in Asia was the Trans-Pacific Partnership (TPP), an agreement among 12 nations representing nearly 40 percent of global GDP. Both Donald Trump and Bernie Sanders vehemently contested this agreement. And after President Trump took office, it was abandoned.[221] Let's examine why.

Firstly, the TPP's secrecy. Like the initial Iranian Nuclear Deal negotiations, most of the TPP negotiations were done in secret. Hence, the American public was unaware of the agreement's contents. According to truthout.org, "intellectual property concerns surrounding the deal and the TPP cannot be reversed or amended without the ratification from all 12 members." On July 8, 2016, Deena Zaidi, author for *Truthout,* wrote:

> While the TPP benefits are mentioned broadly on the website, a leaked classified document posted by WikiLeaks highlights intellectual property concerns. It observes that under the TPP deal, foreign firms will be allowed to "sue" governments for "unlimited compensation." Such arrangements could raise environmental and legal issues, leading to a conflict between domestic and international interests. Moreover, once adopted, TPP cannot be reversed or amended without the approval of all of its 12 member nations.[222]

Secondly, the TPP would benefit multinational corporations while diminishing the American workforce. This trend was notable when one examined the lobbying expenditures of those favoring the TPP. And thirdly, there were serious environmental concerns. The TPP received over 500 anti-TPP petitions from environmental groups that stated:

> The TPP and [Transatlantic Trade and Investment Partnership] would more than double the number of fossil fuel corporations that could follow TransCanada's example and challenge U.S. policies in private tribunals.[223]

Lastly, and most importantly, was its threat to American domestic policy. According to *Truthout*, former President Obama stated that the Trans-Pacific Partnership would benefit "farmers, ranchers, and manufacturers by eliminating more than 18,000 taxes that various countries put on our products."

We saw how well that benefit worked out between the European Union and the United Kingdom—they're still reeling from BREXIT.

Bernie Sanders also noted that the TPP "follows failed trade deals with Mexico, China and other low-wage countries that have cost millions of jobs and shut down tens of thousands of factories across the United States." And he is correct.

Failed trade deals like NAFTA have exploited foreign workers with uncensored child labor, low wages, and severe working conditions. They've also put hundreds of thousands of Americans out of work.

An assessment of the TPP economic impact made by the U.S. International Trade Commission (ITC) concluded that the TPP is likely to "have only a small positive effect on U.S. growth." And according to the Public Citizen, the ITC's "faulty methodologies led to overtly optimistic projections." These optimistic projections calculated a U.S. global trade deficit of $21.7 billion by 2032. The ITC believed the deal would "worsen the trade balances of 65 percent of 55 U.S. agriculture, manufacturing and services sectors." Lori Wallach, director of the Public Citizen's Global Trade Watch, stated that the ITC analysis "suggests that if ever implemented, the TPP could be disastrous."[224]

And even though Clinton was fundamentally opposed to the TPP, she was the impetus behind the agreement. Hear what she said:

> This agreement is not just about eliminating trade barriers, which is crucial for boosting U.S. exports and creating jobs here at home. It's also about agreeing on the rules of the road for an integrated Pacific economy that is open, free, transparent, and fair. It will put in place strong protections for workers, the environment, intellectual property, and innovation—all critical American values.

For an agreement that had the potential to collapse the American domestic market to go as far as being approved by the 12 nations before awaiting ratification by Congress unquestioningly wreaked of another agenda, one which fits nicely into our chapter on borders.

There is much more that can be written about the Asian pivot, but let me sum up its success and failure under the Obama administration in this manner; we made significant inroads in building relations with our Asian partners, all except one—the reason we made the pivot in the first place, China.

Clinton's vision for the Rebalance was a comprehensive policy joining diplomatic, military, and economic engagement—all aimed to deter Chinese expansion. And yet, due to the sequestration of our military, we failed to achieve any actionable deterrence in the South China Sea. China continues expanding and encroaching upon our allies' land and maritime boundaries.

ॐ

China's Nine-Dash Line

China has laid claim to approximately 85% of the maritime boundaries of the South China Sea (SCS), existing since 1947, per the China Nine-Dash Line.[225] The precise coordinates of the nine-dash-line boundaries China claims are not yet public. What was apparent, though, is that while China was land grabbing new islands and laying claim to the territorial waters of American allies like the Philippines, President Obama's relationship with China's President Xi Jinping was deteriorating.

The reasoning for the decline appeared to originate from Obama's dismissal of his "red line" threat in Syria, even after evidence revealed that the Bashar Assad regime was gassing its people. Since then, Xi Jinping knew he could defy the U.S. government and face no consequences.

To underscore his contempt for Obama, at the 2016 G-20 meeting, Xi Jinping "did not extend red-carpet stairs by which Obama could exit the plane after Air Force One landed at Hangzhou."[226]

In contrast, Trump's November 2017 visit to China received not only the red-carpet stairs but also a rare official dinner in the Forbidden City—never before has a U.S. President received such an honor.[227]

To emphasize how upside down our relationship with China had become, during the G-20, "Chinese boats were spotted at Scarborough Shoal, another waterway claimed by the Philippines where the U.S. has warned China not to stake out more artificial islands,"

[228] and the blatant affront to the U.S. was not even addressed.

According to the article, *Obama's Pivot Fails to Deter China*, Eli Lake writes,

> Obama's administration has in the last week encouraged the Philippines to work out the dispute over artificial islands with China on its own, despite the White House's support for a ruling at The Hague in July against China's claims to the waterways.[229]

Here again, the contrast between the Obama-Clinton Asian Pivot and Trump's 2017 Asian revival is staggering. The same Mr. Xi who defied Obama honored Trump and, notably, reigned in any signs of Chinese aggression in the SCS—even if it was only a token gesture.

As I bring this section on the Asian Pivot to a close, let's pause to reflect on another pattern present in the Obama administration—abandoning your allies and leaving them to fend for themselves; which I pointed out regarding Egypt. Obama had a way of getting nations entangled in domestic and foreign disputes and then, instead of leading them through the conflict, he puts the onus of negotiating the outcome upon them. Consider the following:

While sitting in briefings at NATO, I heard the words, "President Obama wants us to take more responsibility," after his Russian reset became Russian expansionism. While sitting in a class on the Arab Spring, I heard the words, "where is America?" after President Obama's Middle East meddling brought down Mubarak in Egypt. After Clinton failed to renegotiate the Status of Forces Agreement (SOFA)[230] needed for the U.S. to continue military support in Iraq, I heard the words, "the U.S. will train the elite Iraqi force to fight ISIS,"[231] as ISIS was growing. And after the death of Muammar al-Gaddafi, we ensured the Libyan nation, "we will help you build a democracy"—only to turn it over to radical insurgents resulting in a civil war. According to U.S. Army General Paul Vallely, "It was Obama and the State Department that created the weapon sale over there, basically arming the Muslim Brotherhood, backed Al-Qaeda radical Islamic elements over there—that created the problem in the first place.[232]"

The Arab Spring, sprung by Obama, is now the Arab Winter. After reviewing the links and connections between Obama, Clinton, their Muslim Brotherhood aides, and White House staff members in conjunction with the Arab Spring, there appeared to be a grander U.S.-Muslim Brotherhood strategy. The ordeal may have been a futile attempt for Obama to help organize the rise of the Muslim Brotherhood in the Middle East. It failed. And in Egypt, home to the Muslim Brotherhood, it failed miserably. Did you know that Egypt felt so betrayed by the United States that it started purchasing its military arms from Russia? That is until Trump took office.

And when Obama's muddled plan for deterrence failed with China, he left our allies to fend for themselves. The outcome of the Obama-Clinton Asian pivot was tenuousness, at the very most. For Trump, it's been a foreign policy nightmare. Few connect North Korea's nuclear threat to Obama's failed Asian Pivot, which played an essential role in China's ineffective intervention on behalf of the North Korean crisis.

God forbid if Trump's administration could not thwart China's aggression against our allies or a North Korean nuke.

Of the Asian pivot, *five-thirty-eight* sums it up this way:

In addition to economic considerations, these strategic concerns are a primary reason why, as Obama put it in his November 2011 speech before the Australian Parliament, "the United States will play a larger and long-term role in shaping this region and its future."[233]

On the security front, despite headlines over the past few years dominated by Russian adventurism in Ukraine, Iran's nuclear program, and the rise of the Islamic State group, it is China—a rapidly rising power seeking to carve out a global leadership role for itself —that poses a challenge to both U.S. military preeminence and global leadership. China's large-scale land reclamation and aggressive patrolling in disputed waters in the South China Sea have sparked concerns about Beijing's desire to reshape the Asia-Pacific region to suit its needs better.[234]

After Trump was elected, he took a call from Taiwan President Tsai lng-wen. She congratulated him, and they discussed strengthening U.S.-Taiwan relations. The State Department was furious, among others. Why? Because Trump just stepped on another cockatrice egg that had existed since the Nixon administration in 1979 when we dumped Taiwan for China. Now that you have a general idea about the China Nine-Dash Line let me ask, "Do you think Donald Trump was out of line when he spoke to the Taiwanese President or was he getting America back in line to protect our allies?" One call and the China Nine-Dash Line may have just lost a few dashes.

⁊

The Four Years before Trump

Let's reflect on a few events that transpired during the last four years of Obama's presidency.

First, there was the American soldier who was detained indefinitely in Mexico. Next, there were the American hostages in Iran—you know, the ones we paid Iran to release.

Now, we shouldn't mind if our country pays for the release of an American, but only if we leverage are options. Sadly, our government went through the entire process of negotiating a nuclear deal with an avowed enemy of the United States and Israel and never exercised its right to leverage sanctions for swapping our hostages.

Another instance revolved around a soldier who was told to stand down after reporting the rape of young boys by older

Afghani men at our American base in Afghanistan. Night after night, our government subjected the conscience of our young military men to the screams of these boys. Can you imagine?

This is the trail of injustice that follows a government that takes bribes. It causes them to lose all moral footing, leaving our brave men and women to stand against evil alone.

At one time, America was considered a righteous nation leading the world; what happened?

I am reminded of the scripture, "when the righteous are in control, the people rejoice when the wicked lead the people hide." Oh, where oh, where did our righteousness go? Well, not far. The fact that Trump challenged the corrupt status quo in Washington has emboldened the fight for justice—it even caused foreign leaders to reassess their moral integrity. Powerful.

One last memory of Obama's last four years—the humiliation America faced when caught spying on our allies, from Merkel to Netanyahu.

Whether realized or not, these events shaped public opinion, and not in a positive way. We watched former President Obama draw Red Lines, Green Lines, and No lines. The blurring of these lines left our allies concerned about their national security, and Israel threatened on all sides as Iran grew its terrorist network and nuclear arsenal.

While writing this chapter in November 2016, I overheard the Filipino President tell former President Obama to "go to hell" on the Filipino news. My heart bled. Do you comprehend the significance of that? Can you believe this is what world leaders thought of President Obama's worldview?

One year later, in November 2017, President Trump returned from a successful twelve-day Asia tour where the United States and the Philippines publicly announced their strong alliance by releasing a joint statement of cooperation on mutual interests and shared regional challenges. Furthermore, the U.S. provided the Philippines with additional funding for counterterrorism, humanitarian needs, military security capabilities, and drug demand reduction programs. That, my friends, is what you call a step in the right direction—wouldn't you agree?

Nevertheless, Trump still had hurdles to jump with our Filipino ally; sadly, Filipino President Duterte turned to Chinese Prime Minister Xi for support after being abandoned by the Obama administration. China hailed its newly found alliance as the "golden period of fast development."

The transference of hegemonic global power from the United States to China escalated during the Obama era and was stalled, if not reversed, under the Trump administration.

Since Biden's appointment, between the Hunter Biden scandal and the ineptness of Biden's foreign policy to effectively keep China from fulfilling its aspirations of the China nine-dash line, hegemonic transference to China has advanced at an alarming rate. China and its Axis, Russia, Iran, and Venezuela are the greatest threat to American interests, democratic advancement, and the balance of military power at the time of this book.

Even though Nancy Pelosi traveled to Taiwan to assure our U.S. ally of our full military support should China invade, the chances of a kumbaya outcome are slim. China continues to intimidate and exercise its One China Vision —a vision which Nancy Pelosi referred to in her blunderous address to the American people after returning from her Asia/Taiwan trip.

American Restoration

When Donald Trump became the President of the United States of America, he stepped onto a global stage desperately looking for the America that led the Free World on the heels of World War II.

That America has led the Free World for the last 70 years and is a remarkable nation replete with extraordinary citizens from the earth's four corners.

Let's peek at what a unified America accomplished in only 3.5 years to bring an end to Hitler and Japanese aggression—it's unparalleled and staggering:

> During the 3.5 years of World War II, starting with the Japanese bombing of Pearl Harbor in December 1941 and ending with the surrender of Germany and Japan in 1945, the U.S. produced 22 aircraft carriers, 8 battleships, 48 cruisers, 349 destroyers, 420 destroyer escorts, 203 submarines, 34 million tons of merchants ships, 100,000 fighter aircraft, 98,00 bombers, 24,000 transport aircraft, 58,000 training aircraft, 93,000

tanks, 257,000 artillery pieces, 105,000 mortars, 3,000,000 machine guns, and 2,500,000 military trucks. America put 16.1 million men into the uniforms of various armed services. We invaded Africa, Sicily, and Italy. We won the battle for the Atlantic, planned and executed D-Day, marched across the Pacific and Europe, developed the atomic bomb, and ultimately ended the wars with Japan and Germany.

At the end of 2020, our allies were basking in a revived hope that America would be there for them. President Trump restored economic stability and respect in both the Domestic and International arenas.

Before President Trump took office, America was in decline, which put the whole world in danger. At the forefront of its downfall were George Soros, former President Obama, and former Secretary Clinton—and as we've seen, they are not going away. But neither are we, the American people.

Now with President Biden at the helm of the land of the brave and home of the free, constitutional liberties are eroding at a striking pace. The American dream is being replaced with elite socialism, and Americans live in a state of increased insecurity, confusion, and fear of the future.

If the America that rallied around Obama's slogan for "change" would change from its wicked ways, shed racial bias, hatred, and all forms of division caused by self and selfish interests, and come together for the common good of God and America there is no telling what we can accomplish.

And I close with these words:

"Our transport is stuck at the airport; the Libyan government is not answering. What about ours? No answer, but I am working on it."

Twelve hours after Ambassador Chris Steven and his compound were attacked, the CIA director in Benghazi still couldn't get ahold of Washington. Where was our Secretary of State, our President, our Commander-in-Chief? We're talking about a staffed American CIA compound under siege, and no one answered the phone in Washington? That's right, no one answered. Why? They were too busy spinning spider webs, hatching cockatrice eggs, and releasing vipers.

℁

Closing Thoughts

Since the 2016 election, the media has vilified President Trump daily. No other President has faced such baseless hatred and relentless opposition. While updating this book, I came across a continual stream of journalism that twisted and misrepresented Trump's vision, intent, and efforts to Make American Great Again. Why?

Notably, the diverse narratives of this book and all the protests over Trump's nationalism are directly and indirectly connected to the Soros-Obama-Clinton Network. So, of course, I won't leave you hanging—stay tuned for my next book to be released soon, *Convergence*.

One by one, the dominos fall. False witnesses come and go. Judges, politicians, and employees of the United States Government are bribed to dig up dirt, destroy Trump's reputation, file inflammatory charges and create smokescreens like the Trump Dossier, Mar Lago, and most recently, a family fraud scandal. All were designed to keep the public's attention on Trump and off the seditious members of both the Democratic and Republican parties. They desire to dismantle the Constitutional foundations of America.

From Benghazi to Uranium One—Podesta emails to Wasserman-Schultz's IT scandal, there is a trail of betrayal and corruption beyond this book's scope. The future of President Trump and the United States of America is in the balance.

The Network of George Soros is working overtime to drive nihilism and a new order in America based on the Universal Declaration of Human Rights. This godless elite document has given license to lascivious leaders at the expense of a nation's moral collective conscience.

It's up to the American people to be informed and choose the path of life. This was the choice given to Israel by God:

৪৩

Write me at hadas@hadassahjacobs.com

Check out my website and courses:

www.hadassahjacobs.com

Follow me on . . .

Twitter:

Https://twitter.com/hadasonpolitics

Make sure to write a review on Amazon!

Your *Thank You* gift for reading my book is waiting for you! Subscribe to www.hadassahjacobs.com and receive it today!

ACKNOWLEDGEMENTS

This book would not have been possible without the guidance and support of Dr. Alan Berger of the Holocaust Department at Florida Atlantic University, Yael Granot, who was the Director of the Holocaust Studies Department of Haifa University, and Dan Shueftan, the director of the National Security Studies Program; who deserves a special mention.

Twenty years ago, you were a guest speaker for a three-day conference on Israeli National Security hosted by the Chicago Jewish Federation. You taught a presentation on terrorism that I never forgot. During the presentation, I leaned over to my friend and said, "we're going to Haifa to study with Dan Shueftan."

Who knew those words would land me at the University of Haifa twenty years later? Thank you, Dan, for the call and for accepting me into the program—it changed my life.

To Rachel Suissa, my professor who took the time to read many chapters in this book and write a review. Thank you for your guidance through the deep waters of Middle Eastern theory has opened me to a whole new world of understanding.

To my mentor, Brendon Burchard. I thank God for connecting me with you and your life's work to help others succeed. Your influence is the single most important reason this book exists. Your high performance and marketing training has changed how I structure my ideas, goals, time, and talents. What a game-changer you are and continue to be in my life. Thanks, Brendon!

Lastly, to my dear friend Bill Mehlman of blessed memory. Bill was a prolific author, editor, and columnist who set the bar for excellence in journalism. I have yet to meet anyone who writes with the clarity of purpose and mastery of words like you, Bill. A Divine gift so fittingly placed in the hands of a humble man. Thank you, Bill, for your ideas and encouragement throughout the writing of this book. May your love for America, Israel, and the Almighty be rewarded!

"We are not now that strength which in the old days moved earth and heaven. That which we are, we are. One equal temper of heroic hearts made weak by time and fate, but strong in will to strive, to seek, to find and not to yield."

Alfred Tennyson

ଓ

ABOUT THE AUTHOR

At 50, Hadas returned to college after working in the field of U.S.-Israel relations since early 2000.

She graduated Magna Cum Laude from Florida Atlantic University with a B.A. in Jewish Studies and History. In 2017, she completed her MA degree in National Security Studies from Haifa University, Israel.

Today, Hadas lives in Israel. She is an author, course creator, entrepreneur, and expert in global ideological trends and strategic messaging.

She is working towards her Ph.D. while aiding organizations in their fight against antisemitism and ideological trends that undermine the ethos of Israel and the U.S.

*" If you tell the truth,
you don't have to remember anything."*

Mark Twain

NOTES

[1] Isaiah 59:8

[2] Isaiah 59:14-15

[3] Fastest striking snake
http://www.animaldanger.com/australia.php

[4] ibid.

[5] Steiner, Amanda M. (2015, June 29). Your Fired: NBC Drops Miss Universe *and Miss USA After Donald Trump's Comments About Mexican Immigrants.* Retrieved from http://www.people.com/article/nbc-drops-donald-trump-miss-universe-miss-usa

[6] Boston, Claire. (2015, July 2). *Serta Will Stop Selling Trump Mattress Line In Latest Defection.* Retrieved from http://www.bloomberg.com/politics/articles/2015-07-01/serta-will-stop-selling-trump-mattress-line-in-latest-defection

[7] Walker, Hunter. (2015, July 6). *Donald Trump just released an epic statement raging against Mexican immigrants and 'disease.'* Retrieved from

http://www.businessinsider.com/donald-trumps-epic-statement-on-mexico-2015-7

[8] Carusone, Angelo. *Tell Macy's: Dump Donald Trump*. Retrieved from http://petitions.moveon.org/sign/urge-macys-to-dump-donald

[9] Nimmo, Kurt. (2016, March 12). *Soros funded moveone.org takes credit for violence in Chicago*. Retrieved from http://www.infowars.com/soros-funded-moveon-org-takes-credit-for-violence-in-chicago/

[10] Kiely, Eugene. (2012, April 19). *The Facts About 'Fat Cats.'* Retrieved from http://www.factcheck.org/2012/04/the-facts-about-fat-cats/

[11] http://www.politifact.com/personalities/moveon/

[12] Definition: the undermining of the power and authority of an established system or institution: *the ruthless subversion of democracy* | *[count noun]: subversions of conventional morality*.

Even the post-election change.org petition, "Electoral[13] College: Make Hillary Clinton on December 19" has his signature all over it. Frye, Patrick. (2016, March 13). *George Soros— Funded moveon.org Takes Responsibility For Violent Donald Trump Protest—Promises More Protests To Come.* Retrieved from http://www.inquisitr.com/2885453/george-soros-funded-moveon-org-takes-responsibility-for-violent-donald-trump-protest promises-more-protests-are-to-come

[14] McClure-Davidson, Vicki. (2010, September 7). *Profile of a Liberal Sociopath: Billionaire George Soros Helped Nazis Murder & Steal From Jews, Feels No Remorse or Guilt.* Retrieved from http://www.frugal-cafe.com/public_html/frugal-blog/frugal-cafe-blogzone/2010/09/07/profile-of-a-liberal-sociopath-billionaire-george-soros-helped-nazis-murder-steal-from-jews-feels-no-remorse-or-guilt/

[15] McClure Davidson, Vicki. (2011, January 28th). *George Soros Says He Feels No Remorse For Collaborating With Nazis During WWII to Send His Fellow Jews to the Death Camps, Steal Their Property.* Retrieved from http://itmakessenseblog.com/2011/01/28/george-soros-says-he-feels-no-remorse-for-collaborating-with-nazis-during-wwii-to-send-his-fellow-jews-to-the-death-camps-steal-their-property/

[16] Geller, Pamella. (2006, October 30). *The Judenrat Soros.* Retrieved from http://pamelageller.com/2006/10/the_judenrat_so-1.html/ In an interview with 60 minutes Soros, responding to a statement of him watching lots of Jews get shipped off to death camps, said,"Right. I was 14 years old. And I would say that that's when my character was made."

[17] http://message.snopes.com/showthread.php?t=43876

[18] Geller, Pamella. (2006, October 11). *Soros and the Nazis Undermining the Jewish People.* Retrieve from http://pamelageller.com/2006/10/soros_and_the_n.html/

19 Geller, Pamella. (2006, October 11). *Soros and the Nazis Undermining the Jewish People*. Retrieved from http://pamelageller.com/2006/10/soros_and_the_n.html/#sthash.3WQ64AGG.dpuf

20 Geller, Pamella. (2006, October 11). *Soros and the Nazis Undermining the Jewish People*. Retrieved from http://pamelageller.com/2006/10/soros_and_the_n.html/#sthash.3WQ64AGG.dpuf

21 Cyber Berkut. https://www.bbc.com/news/blogs-trending-41915295

22 Druden, Tyler. (2015, July 2). Hacked Emails Expose George Soros As Ukraine Puppet Master. Retrieved from http://www.zerohedge.com/news/2015-06-01/hacked-emails-expose-george-soros-ukraine-puppet-master

23 Browne, Clayton. (2015, May 20). *Soros Says China Is A Major Risk For World War 3*. Retrieved from http://www.valuewalk.com/2015/05/soros-china-is-risk-for-world-war-3/

24 Druden, Tyler. (2015, May 22). *George Soros Warns, "No Exaggeration" That China-US On "Threshold of World War3."* Retrieved from http://www.zerohedge.com/news/2015-05-21/george-soros-warns-no-exaggeration-china-us-threshold-world-war-3

[25] Parry, Robert. (2016, April 5). *'Corruption' as a Propoganda Weapon.* Retreived from http://www.globalresearch.ca/corruption-as-a-propaganda-weapon/5518663

[26] Corcoran, Kieran. (2015, January 16). *Billionaire George Soros spent 33 million bankrolling Ferguson demonstrators create 'echo chamber' drive national protests.* Retrieved from http://www.dailymail.co.uk/news/article-2913625/Billionaire-George-Soros-spent-33MILLION-bankrolling-Ferguson-demonstrators-create-echo-chamber-drive-national-protests.html#ixzz4EqPYLzLT

[27] Riddell, Kelly. (2015, January 14). *George Soros funds Ferguson protests, hopes to spur civil action.* Retrieved from http://www.washingtontimes.com/news/2015/jan/14/george-soros-funds-ferguson-protests-hopes-to-spur/

[28] Riddell, Kelly. (2015, January 14). *George Soros funds Ferguson protests, hopes to spur civil action.* Retrieved from http://www.washingtontimes.com/news/2015/jan/14/george-soros-funds-ferguson-protests-hopes-to-spur/

[29] Teshuva means, "to return." Specifically, taking words or an answer to your actions and retuning to God.

[30] Kenton, Will. *The Panama Papers: what you should know.* Investopedia, updated June 12, 2022. https://www.investopedia.com/terms/p/panama-papers.asp

---

[31] Editor. (2016, April 5). *Geopolitiks of Corruption: George Soros and the 'Panama Leaks.'* Retrieved from http://www.theeventchronicle.com/panama-papers/geopolitics-corruption-george-soros-panama-leaks/#

[32] Highlighted in the Panama Paper leaks were Russia's Vladimir Putin indirectly, and more specifically his best friend, Sergei Roldugin. Also taken to task were the father of British Prime Minister David Cameron, Argentinian President Mauricio Macri (who is pro-American) and former Presidents Cristina and Nestor Kirchner. The list continues with Ukranian and Azerbejain Presidents Poroshenko and Aliyev, Saudi King Salaman, former Emir of Qatar, and current President of the United Arab Emirates. It also included the former Prime Minister of China and several other large Chinese officials.

[33] Editor. (2016, April 5). *Geopolitiks of Corruption: George Soros and the 'Panama Leaks.'* Retrieved from http://www.theeventchronicle.com/panama-papers/geopolitics-corruption-george-soros-panama-leaks/#

[34] .https://answers.yahoo.com/question/index?qid=201008261 72157AA3mewa

[35] Other reports mark the recent visit of George Soros with Robert Malley as his 13th time. Watson, Steve. (2016, March 2). *Soros Met With Obama's top ISIS Advisor Last Month.* Retrieved from http://www.infowars.com/soros-met-with-obamas-top-isis-advisor-last-month-2/

[36]Rob Malley's tenure will end in January 2017 when President elect Trump replaces the Obama administration.

[37] Safian, Alex. (2015, March 11). *Robert Malley and US Policy on Israel.* Retrieved from http://www.camera.org/index.asp?x_context=8&x_nameinne ws=88&x_article=2962

[38] https://en.wikipedia.org/wiki/Robert_Malley

[39] Watson, Steve. (2016, March 2). *Soros Met With Obama's top ISIS Advisor Last Month.* Retrieved from http://www.infowars.com/soros-met-with-obamas-top-isis-advisor-last-month-2/

[40] Sainato, Michael. (2016, August 15). *DC Leak Exposes Top Clinton Donor George Soros Manipulating Elections.* Retrieved from http://observer.com/2016/08/dc-leak-exposes-top-clinton-donor-george-soros-manipulating-elections/

[41] Ehrenfeld, Rachel, Macomber, Shawn. (2004, October 4). Rachel Ehrenfeld is the author of "Funding Evil" (Bonus Books, 2003). Shawn Macomber is a staff writer at the American Spectator. *George Soros: The 'God' Who Carries Around Some Dangerous Demons.* Retrieved from http://articles.latimes.com/2004/oct/04/opinion/oe-ehrenfeld4

[42] *"Kate's Law" and the License To Hate.* (2016, April 27). Retrieved from http://www.huffingtonpost.com/samanta-honigman/kates-law-and-the-license_b_9789508.html

[43] Karlamangla, Soumya. (2022, Sept. 22) *Gavin Newsom Rejected These 5 Bills.*
https://www.nytimes.com/2022/09/27/us/gavin-newsom-veto-bills.html

[44] Homeland Security. (2009, July 21) *ICE. Secure Communities: A Comprehensive Plan to Identify and Remove Criminal Aliens (Strategic Plan).* Retrieved from
https://www.ice.gov/doclib/foia/secure_communities/securec
ommunitiesstrategicplan09.pdf

[45] Preston. Julia. (2009, November 12) *U.S. Identifies 111,000 Immigrants With Criminal Records.* Retrieved from
http://www.nytimes.com/2009/11/13/us/13ice.html

[46] Homeland Security. (2009, July 21) *ICE. Secure Communities: A Comprehensive Plan to Identify and Remove Criminal Aliens (Strategic Plan).* Retrieved from
https://www.ice.gov/doclib/foia/secure_communities/securec
ommunitiesstrategicplan09.pdf

[47] Preston, Julia. (2011, August 13). *Resistance Widens to Obama Initiative on Criminal Immigrants.*
http://www.nytimes.com/2011/08/13/us/politics/13secure.htm
l?_r=1&ref=us

[48] Thau, David. (2012, January) *Immigration and the Failure of Federalism.* Journal of Civil Rights and Economic Development: Issue 2 Volume 26, Winter 2012, Issue 2. p. 518. "[T]he National Immigration and Customs Enforcement Council-an AFL-CIO affiliate-and affiliated local councils cast a unanimous 259-0 vote of no confidence in ICE Director

John Morton and Assistant Director Phyllis Coven." Retrieval from
http://scholarship.law.stjohns.edu/cgi/viewcontent.cgi?article =1708&context=jcred

[49] Seper, Jerry. (2010, August 9). *Agents' union disavows leaders of ICE.* Retrieved from
http://www.washingtontimes.com/news/2010/aug/9/agents-union-disavows-leaders-of-ice/

[50] Homeland Security. (2009, July 21) *ICE. Secure Communities: A Comprehensive Plan to Identify and Remove Criminal Aliens (Strategic Plan).* Retrieved from
https://www.ice.gov/doclib/foia/secure_communities/securec ommunitiesstrategicplan09.pdf

[51]Preston, Julia. (2012, January 7). *Agents' Union Stalls Training on Deportation Rules. Retrieved from*
http://www.nytimes.com/2012/01/08/us/illegal-immigrants-who-commit-crimes-focus-of-deportation.html?pagewanted=all

[52] Steinlight, Stephen. (2012, January 11). *National ICE Council Freezes the Obama Blitz.* Center for Immigration Studies. http://cis.org/steinlight/national-ICE-council-freezes-the-obama-blitz

[53] Pear, Robert. (2011, August 18). *Fewer Youths to Be Deported in New Policy.* Retrieved from
http://www.nytimes.com/2011/08/19/us/19immig.html

54 BBC News. (2011, August 18) *US Will Review 300,000 Immigration Deportation Cases*. Retrieved from http://www.bbc.co.uk/news/world-us-canada-14585238

55 Synder, Michael. (2013, August 19). *Obama Administration Makes Secret Deal With Mexico To Help Illegal Immigrants In The Workplace*. Retrieved from http://endoftheamericandream.com/archives/obama-administration-makes-secret-deal-with-mexico-to-help-illegal-immigrants-in-the-workplace

56 Grandoni, Dino. (2011, September 9). *Obama Administration Nears Its Millionth Deportation*, The Atlantic Wire. Retrieved from http://www.thewire.com/national/2011/09/obama-administration-nears-its-millionth-deportation/42302/

57 Manuel, Jens, Passel J., Cohn, D. (2016, November 3). *5 facts about illegal immigration in the U.S.* Retrieved from http://www.pewresearch.org/fact-tank/2015/11/19/5-facts-about-illegal-immigration-in-the-u-s/

58 Chambers, Francesca. (2016, June 30). *Obama launches an extraordinary rant against Trump's 'xenophobia' and 'disregard for workers' - as he insists 'I care about poor people'*. Retrieved from http://www.dailymail.co.uk/news/article-3666104/Obama-s-anti-Trump-huddles-Mexican-leader-compared-Republican-Hitler-Canada-s-liberal-pin-mocked-Clinton-rival.html#ixzz4DTH77zUr

59 Adam Liptak. (2012, June 25). *Blocking Parts of Arizona Law, Justices Allow Its Centerpiece*. Retrieved From

http://www.nytimes.com/2012/06/26/us/supreme-court-rejects-part-of-arizona-immigration-law.html

[60] Adam Liptak. (2012, June 25). *Blocking Parts of Arizona Law, Justices Allow Its Centerpiece.* Retrieved From http://www.nytimes.com/2012/06/26/us/supreme-court-rejects-part-of-arizona-immigration-law.html

[61] Adam Liptak. (2012, June 25). *Blocking Parts of Arizona Law, Justices Allow Its Centerpiece.* Retrieved From http://www.nytimes.com/2012/06/26/us/supreme-court-rejects-part-of-arizona-immigration-law.html

[62] Adam Liptak. (2012, June 25). *Blocking Parts of Arizona Law, Justices Allow Its Centerpiece.* Retrieved From http://www.nytimes.com/2012/06/26/us/supreme-court-rejects-part-of-arizona-immigration-law.html

[63] Radia, Kirit. (2013, April 20). *Boston Bomb Suspect Alarmed Russian Relatives With Extremist Views.* Retrieved from http://abcnews.go.com/US/boston-bomb-suspect-alarmed-russian-relatives-extremist-views/story?id=19006449

[64] Buncombe, Andrew. (2016, June 19). *Donald Trump Says US Should Consider Profiling Muslims.* Retrieved from http://www.independent.co.uk/news/world/americas/us-elections/donald-trump-says-us-should-consider-profiling-muslims-a7090731.html

[65] http://www.foxnews.com/us/2017/11/01/nyc-terror-attack-leaves-8-dead-several-injured-suspects-notes-pledged-isis-loyalty.html

66 https://heavy.com/news/2017/10/sayfullo-saipov-manhattan-truck-ramming-suspect-terror/

67 http://www.nj.com/passaic-county/index.ssf/2017/11/south_paterson_unleashes_on_anim al_ny_terror_suspect_as_fbi_swarms_community.html

68 https://www.donaldjtrump.com/positions/pay-for-the-wall

69 https://www.fincen.gov/statutes_regs/patriot/

70 http://www.foxnews.com/politics/2017/09/21/trumps-border-wall-look-at-numbers.html

71 Colangelo, Lisa, Pearson, E. (2016, April 23). *Immigrants from Dominican Republic, Ecuador share their Citizenship NOW! success stories*. Retrieved from http://www.nydailynews.com/new-york/immigrants-share-citizenship-success-stories-article-1.2612116

72 written by Kim Johnson

73 Brown, Tim. (2015, May 11). *1,063 Documented Examples of Barack Obama's Lying, Lawbreaking, Corruption, Cronyism, Hypocrisy, Waste, Etc.* Retrieved from http://freedomoutpost.com/1063-documented-examples-of-barack-obamas-lying-lawbreaking-corruption-cronyism-hypocrisy-waste-etc/

74 Alman, Daniel. (2009-2016, May). *1,304 well sourced examples of Barack Obama's lying, lawbreaking, corruption, cronyism, hypocrisy, waste, etc.* Retrieved from https://danfromsquirrelhill.wordpress.com/2013/08/15/obama-252/

[75] http://www.wikihow.com/Spot-a-Pathological-Liar

[76] Hill, Tamara. *6 Subtle Characteristics of The Pathological Liar*. Retrieved from http://blogs.psychcentral.com/caregivers/2014/09/6-subtle-characteristics-of-the-pathological-liar/

[77] Johnson, Charles, C. (2016, July 6). *CONFIRMED: Bloods Gangbanger, Democrat #AltonSterling Owned Illegal Gun, Had Drug, Assault Weapon Convictions*. Retrieved from http://gotnews.com/confirmed-bloods-gangbanger-altonsterling-owned-illegal-gun-drug-gun-convictions/

[78] McBride, Jessica. (2016, July 6). *Alton Sterling Arrest Record, Criminal History & Rap Sheet [DOCUMENTS]*. Retrieved from http://heavy.com/news/2016/07/alton-sterling-arrest-record-criminal-history-rap-sheet-sex-offender-sex-offense-crime-baton-rouge-louisiana-police-shooting-blane-salamoni-howie-lake-shot-charges-video-youtube-facebook-watch/

[79] Hill, Tamara. *6 Subtle Characteristics of The Pathological Liar*. Retrieved from http://blogs.psychcentral.com/caregivers/2014/09/6-subtle-characteristics-of-the-pathological-liar/

[80] Alman, Daniel. (2009-2016, May). *1,304 well sourced examples of Barack Obama's lying, lawbreaking, corruption, cronyism, hypocrisy, waste, etc*. Retrieved from https://danfromsquirrelhill.wordpress.com/2013/08/15/obama-252/

[81] https://web.archive.org/web/20101119082141/http://www.washingtonexaminer.com/politics/Former-lobbyists-in-senior-Obama-administration-positions-83362902.html#ixzz4FXWe0xzY This article may require a password or sign up with the Washington Examiner. Articles that confirm this information include endnote 73. Here are two other "must reads" if you are interested in this lobby issues by Timothy Carney: Retrieved from http://www.washingtonexaminer.com/article/2562038 and http://www.washingtonexaminer.com/obama-hires-revolving-door-lobbyist-and-clinton-fixer-john-podesta/article/2540496

[82] Carney, Timothy. (2013, July 23). *Obama administration packed with lobbyists he vowed not to hire.* Retrieved from http://www.washingtonexaminer.com/obama-administration-packed-with-lobbyists-he-vowed-not-to-hire/article/2533397 Carney and McGrath cite over 100 lobbyists hired during the Obama Administration.

[83] https://www.activistfacts.com/organizations/528-center-for-american-progress/

[84] Sargent, Greg. (2009, March 10). *Center For American Progress Launching Big War Room To Drive Obama Agenda.* Retrieved from http://www.sourcewatch.org/index.php/Center_for_American_Progress

[85] Alman, Daniel. (2009-2016, May). *1,304 well sourced examples of Barack Obama's lying, lawbreaking, corruption, cronyism, hypocrisy, waste, etc.*

https://danfromsquirrelhill.wordpress.com/2013/08/15/obama-252/

[86] Alman, Daniel. (2009-2016, May). *1,304 well sourced examples of Barack Obama's lying, lawbreaking, corruption, cronyism, hypocrisy, waste, etc.* Items 501 through 1,000 can be found at https://danfromsquirrelhill.wordpress.com/2015/12/04/obama-part-2/

[87] Alman, Daniel. (2009-2016, May). *1,304 well sourced examples of Barack Obama's lying, lawbreaking, corruption, cronyism, hypocrisy, waste, etc.* Items 1,001 through 1,249 can be found at https://danfromsquirrelhill.wordpress.com/2015/12/04/obama-part-3/

[88] Deuteronomy 1:15-16, "So I took the chief of your tribes, wise men, and known, and made them heads over you, captains over thousands, and captains over hundreds, and captains over fifties, and captains over tens, and officers among your tribes. And I charged your judges at that time, saying Hear the causes between your brethren, and judge righteously between every man ands brother, and the stranger that is with him."

[89] Deuteronomy 11:24-25

[90] The book of Jeremiah chapter 31

[91] https://www.archives.gov/founding-docs

[92] Hormandi, Dan. (2014, April 30). *George Washington's Covenant with God.* Retrieved from

https://lessonsfromthefounders.wordpress.com/2014/04/30/289/

[93] https://www.billofrightsinstitute.org/founding-documents/bill-of-rights/

[94] Spalding, Matthew. Eberly, D., Gregg, S., Loconte, J. Building *a Culture of Character*. Retrieved from http://www.heritage.org/research/lecture/building-a-culture-of-character

[95] Spalding, Matthew. Eberly, D., Gregg, S., Loconte, J. *Building a Culture of Character*. Retrieved from http://www.heritage.org/research/lecture/building-a-culture-of-character

[96] http://www.diffen.com/difference/Anti-Federalist_vs_Federalist

[97] https://www.billofrightsinstitute.org/founding-documents/bill-of-rights/

[98] Kopstein Jeffrey, Lichbach, M. (2000). *Comparative Politics: Interests, Identities, and Institutions in a Changing Global Order*. Cambridge UP. p. 72. Retrieved from https://www.scribd.com/doc/55305065/Comparative-Politics-Interests-Identities-and-Institutions

[99] McLean, Iain. *Thomas Jefferson, John Adams, and the Déclaration des Droits de l'Homme et du Citoyen* in *The future of liberal democracy: Thomas Jefferson and the contemporary world* (Palgrave Macmillan, 2004) online Retrieved from

http://www.palgraveconnect.com/pc/doifinder/10.1057/97814 03981455

[100] Benjamin Franklin (2003). *The Political Thought of Benjamin Franklin.* Edited by Ralph Ketcham; Hackett Publishing. p. 398. Available at https://www.hackettpublishing.com/the-political-thought-of-benjamin-franklin

[101] *The Declaration of the Rights of Man and of the Citizen.* Retrieved from http://avalon.law.yale.edu/18th_century/rightsof.asp

[102] There are those who believe Hegel's idea originated with Immanuel Kant

[103] Georg F. W. Hegel (1770-1831) was a major figure in German idealism.

[104] Popper, Karl R. (1971). *The Open Society, and Its Enemies: The High Tide of Prophecy: Hegel, Marx, and the Aftermath*, 2 vols. 5th rev. ed. Princeton, NJ: Princeton University Press, [1966] 1971, 2:31.

[105] Some scholars dispute the authenticity of Rauschning's recounting of his time with Hitler. Richard Steigmann-Gall considered Rauschning's *Hitler Speaks* (1939), published in America as *The Voice of Destruction*, "to be fraudulent." (*The Holy Reich: Nazi Conceptions of Christianity, 1919-1945* [New York: Cambridge University Press, 2003], 29). There doesn't seem to be anything out of character in what Rauschning wrote. Hitler did do away with the Ten Commandments. Hitler was at war with the Old Testament.

Others saw the true Hitler before Rauschning. See Cardinal Faulhaber, *Judaism, Christianity and Germany* (London: Burns Oates & Washbourne Ltd., 1934). Then there are the public statements of Martin Bormann (1900-1945?), head of the Party Chancellery and Hitler's private secretary: "National Socialist and Christian concepts are incompatible. . . . Our National Socialist world view stands on a much higher level than the concepts of Christianity, which in their essentials were taken over from Judaism. For this reason, too, we can do without Christianity." (Martin Bormann, "National Socialist and Christian Concepts Are Incompatible" [1937], *Nazi Culture: Intellectual, Cultural andSocial Life in the Third Reich*, George L. Mosse [New York: Grosset & Dunlap, 1968], 244). Retrieved from http://www.rightlydividingtheword.com/articles/battle_agains t_the_ten_commandments.htm

[106] Rauschning, "Preface," xiii. *The Ten Commandments: Ten Short Novels of Hitler's War Against The Moral Code. New York*: Simon and Schuester, 1943. Hitler's statement was recounted by Rauschning while spending the evening with him and other Nazi party loyalists at the Reich Chancery. Retrieved from http://www.rightlydividingtheword.com/articles/battle_agains t_the_ten_commandments.htm

[107] Herbert Huffmon, (2004) *The Fundamental Code Illustrated: The Third Commandment, in The Ten Commandments: The Reciprocity of Faithfulness,* ed. William P. Brown., pp. 205–212. Westminster John Knox Press. *The author added additional text for continuity of thought.*

[108] Romans 13:8-10

[109] Rauschning, Hermann (1887- 1982), was a German Conservative Revolutionary who broke with the Nazi party and fled from Germany in 1936. He served as a German officer in WWI and spent the years of WWII denouncing Hitler and the Nazi agenda.

[110] Mann, Thomas, et.al. *The Ten Commandments: Ten Short Novels of Hitler's War Against The Moral Code. New York*: Simon and Schuester, 1943

[111] http://time.com/3508291/china-underground-churches-catholicism-catholics-christianity-christians-kevin-frayer/

[112] http://www.jewishtimesasia.org/shanghai/262-shanghai-communities/46-shanghai-china-jewish-community

[113] Torah is the first five books of the Bible. It lays the foundation of God's government in the earth and His moral laws to govern humanity in a just and righteous manner.

[114] *1968: The Year That Changed History*. Retrieved from https://www.theguardian.com/observer/gallery/2008/jan/17/1

[115] http://www.historynet.com/vietnam-war

[116] Tet Offensive

[117] 1968: Timeline. Retrieved from http://cds.library.brown.edu/projects/1968/reference/timeline.html

118 1968: Timeline. Retrieved from http://cds.library.brown.edu/projects/1968/reference/timeline.html

119 Torry, Jack. (2008, March 30). *Chaotic 1968 Changed America Forever*. Retrieved from http://www.dispatch.com/content/stories/insight/2008/03/30/1968.ART_ART_03-30-08_G1_JL9OP2U.html

120 Kurlansky, Mark. (2004). *1968: the Year that Rocked the World*. Available at https://www.amazon.com/1968-Year-That-Rocked-World/dp/0345455827

121 Rauschning, "Preface," xiii. *The Ten Commandments: Ten Short Novels of Hitler's War Against The Moral Code*. New York: Simon and Schuester, 1943. Hitler's statement was recounted by Rauschning while spending the evening with him and other Nazi party loyalists at the Reich Chancery.

122 Browne, Clayton. (2015, May 20). *Soros Says China Is Major Risk For World War 3*. Retrieved from http://www.valuewalk.com/2015/05/soros-china-is-risk-for-world-war-3/

123 *The Washington Post*, "Center for American Progress, poised to wield influence over 2016, reveals its top donors," January 21, 2015

124 *Politico*, "W.H., CAP to counter Podesta attacks," December 12, 2013

125 ibid.

[126] Isaiah 10:14

[127] Miller, D. (1997). *Sir Karl Raimund Popper, C. H., F. B. A. 28 July 1902--17 September 1994. Elected F.R.S. 1976.* Biographical Memoirs of Fellows of the Royal Society. **43**: 369–310. doi:10.1098/rsbm.1997.0021

[128] Popper archives fasc. 297.11

[129] See also Karl Popper: On freedom. *All life is problem solving* (1999), chapter 7, p. 81f

[130] Soros, George. (1995). *Soros on Soros: Staying Ahead of the Curve.* New York, Wiley. pp. 253-263 Retrieved from http://eu.wiley.com/WileyCDA/WileyTitle/productCd-0471119776.html

[131] Acts 17: 23-28

[132] Popper, Karl. (1947). *The Open Society and Its Enemies: The Spell of Plato. Volume 1*, George Routledge & Sons, ltd., pp. 226, (1971) p. 265. *Complete Volumes I & II* (1966), p. 581

[133] http://shariahthethreat.org/a-short-course-1-what-is-shariah/

[134] http://islam.stackexchange.com/questions/4254/what-is-the-difference-between-hadith-and-Qur'an

[135] Qutb, Sayyid. (2005). *Milestones*, p. Dar al-llm., Damascus, Syria. p. 110-111

[136] There are one or two examples of reformation within Sharia law that appears to allow for a more liberal approach

towards human rights thus appeasing the United Nations Human Rights Council. But don't be fooled. Islamists are allowed to use lying and deceptive techniques to achieve their goals. Hence, even if there is a human rights compromise, the concept of jihad and overthrowing democracy is still the ultimate aim of all that promote Sharia law as compatible within the framework of a national government.

[137] *Shariah: The Threat to America.* Retrieved from https://www.centerforsecuritypolicy.org/upload/wysiwyg/article%20pdfs/Shariah%20-%20The%20Threat%20to%20America%20(Team%20B%20Report)%20Web%2009292010.pdf

[138] Psalm 9:17

[139] Capehart, Jonathan. (2012, June 20). *Pelosi defends her infamous health care remark.* https://www.washingtonpost.com/blogs/post-partisan/post/pelosi-defends-her-infamous-health-care-remark/2012/06/20/gJQAqch6qV_blog.html?utm_term=.68e93afb1d37

[140] ibid.

[141] 2009 figures1,990. Retrieved from http://computationallegalstudies.com/2009/11/08/facts-about-the-length-of-h-r-3962/

[142] Kessler, Glenn. (2013, May 15). *How many pages of regulations for 'Obamacare'?* 2013 numbers range from 20,000 to 33,000. Retrieved from https://www.washingtonpost.com/blogs/fact-

checker/post/how-many-pages-of-regulations-for-obamacare/2013/05/14/61eec914-bcf9-11e2-9b09-1638acc3942e_blog.html

143 Yoo, John. (2016, February 8). *A Call For Action Against Government Overreach*. Retrieved from https://www.aei.org/publication/a-call-for-action-against-government-overreach/

144 Shapiro, Ilya. (2013, December 23). *President Obama's Top 10 Constitutional Violations of 2013*. Retrieved from http://www.forbes.com/sites/realspin/2013/12/23/president-obamas-top-10-constitutional-violations-of-2013/#183f5f7e41bf

145 Shapiro, Ilya. (2015, December 23). *President Obama's Top Ten Constitutional Violations of 2015*. Retrieved from http://www.nationalreview.com/article/428882/obama-violate-constitution-top-ten-2015

146 https://www.oyez.org/cases/2011/11-393 The ACA contained a minimum coverage provision by amending the tax code and providing an individual mandate, stipulating that by 2014, non-exempt individuals who failed to purchase and maintain a minimum level of health insurance must pay a tax penalty. The ACA also contained an expansion of Medicaid, which States had to accept to receive Federal funds for Medicaid, and an employer mandate to obtain health coverage for employees.

147 https://ballotpedia.org/Obamacare_lawsuits

148 https://ballotpedia.org/Obamacare_lawsuits#cite_note-40

---

149 *42 U.S. Code § 2000bb–1 - Free exercise of religion protected.* Retrieved from https://www.law.cornell.edu/uscode/text/42/2000bb-1

150 Bratek, Rebecca. (2104, July 19). *Law firm in Hobby Lobby win is playing key role in religion cases.* Retrieved from http://www.latimes.com/nation/la-na-becket-fund-20140720-story.html

151 Childers, Karl. (2014, March 27). *Hobby Lobby Case Opens TheDoor To Islam Sharia Law Be Careful What Ya Wish.* Retrieved from http://liberalforum.net/viewtopic.php?t=4224&p=211574

152 Clifton, Allen. (2014, July 2). *George Takei: What if Muslims Owned Hobby Lobby and Tried Imposing Sharia Law on Employees?* Retrieved from http://www.forwardprogressives.com/george-takei-muslims-owned-hobby-lobby-tried-forcing-sharia-law-employees/

153 Drobnic Holan, Angie. (2013, May 30). *'Dhimmitude' on page 107 of the health care law exempts Muslims, claims chain email.* Retrieved from http://www.politifact.com/truth-o-meter/statements/2013/may/30/chain-email/dhimmitude-page-107-health-care-law-exempts-muslim/

154 Burns, Eric. (2011, October 13). *Muslims Exempt From Obamacare?* Retrieved from http://www.frontpagemag.com/fpm/108489/muslims-exempt-obamacare-eric-burns

155 ibid.

156 http://obamacarefacts.com/healthcare-sharing-ministry-exemptions/

157 Burns, Eric. (2011, October 13). *Muslims Exempt From Obamacare?* Retrieved from http://www.frontpagemag.com/fpm/108489/muslims-exempt-obamacare-eric-burns

158*AIG Offers First Takaful Homeowners Insurance Product for U.S.* (2008, December 2). Retrieved from http://www.insurancejournal.com/news/national/2008/12/02/95930.htm

159 Macfarlane, Benjamin. *Shariah Compliant Insurance Products – Takaful in the UK.* Retrieved from http://www.bjm-co.com/reports/Article_006_Takaful_150605_101k.pdf

160 *Islamic Finance: Ethics, Concepts, Practice (a summary).* (2014). Retrieved from https://www.cfainstitute.org/learning/foundation/research/Documents/islamic_finance_ethics_concepts_practice.pdf

161 Thajudeen, Kulsanofer Syed. (2012, September). *Branding Takaful: The Issues and Challenges.* INCEIF, The Global University in Islamic Finance. Kuala Lumpur, Malaysia. p.17 Retrieved from https://www.academia.edu/2321516/Branding_Takaful_The_Issues_and_Challenges

162 Hohmann Leo. (2105, July 23). *Major U.S.city poised to implement Islamic law*

Retrieved from http://www.wnd.com/2015/07/major-u-s-city-poised-to-implement-islamic-law/#QO4QxrGme5OXFrKu.99

[163] Bostom, Andrew. (2008).*The Legacy of Jihad*. Prometheus Books, New York.

[164] Maududi, Sayyid. (1992) *The Economic Problems of Man and its Islamic Solution*. Pakistan. 10th edition. p.42 Retrieved from http://www.muslim-library.com/dl/books/English_The_Economic_Problems_of_Man_and_Its_Islamic_Solution.pdf

[165] *Major U.S. City Poised To Implement Islamic Law*. (2016, January 9). Retrieved from http://www.jewsnews.co.il/2016/01/09/major-u-s-city-poised-to-implement-islamic-law-2.html

[166] Maududi, Sayyid. (1992) *The Economic Problems of Man and its Islamic Solution*. Pakistan. 10th edition. p.43 Retrieved from http://www.muslim-library.com/dl/books/English_The_Economic_Problems_of_Man_and_Its_Islamic_Solution.pdf

[167] Maududi, Sayyid. (1992) *The Economic Problems of Man and its Islamic Solution*. Pakistan. 10th edition. p.44 Retrieved from http://www.muslim-library.com/dl/books/English_The_Economic_Problems_of_Man_and_Its_Islamic_Solution.pdf

[168] ibid.

[169] Hanley, Delinda.(2001, January).*In the Wake of 9-11 President Bush and Muslim Leaders Work to Protect Muslim*

Americans. p. 22. Retrieved from
http://www.wrmea.org/2001-november/in-the-wake-of-9-11-
president-bush-and-muslim-leaders-work-to-protect-muslim-
americans.html

[170] Adam, Clymer. (1985, July 14)). *In Short: Nonfiction.*
Retrieved from
http://www.nytimes.com/1985/07/14/books/in-short-
nonfiction-111845.html

[171] a summarized definition of author

[172] Timmerman, Kenneth. (2011, October 21). *Obama
Administration Pulls References to Islam from Terror
Training Materials, Official Says.* Retrieved from
http://dailycaller.com/2011/10/21/obama-administration-
pulls-references-to-islam-from-terror-training-materials-
official-says/

[173] Al-Marayati, Salam. (2011, October 19). *The Wrong Way
to Fight Terrorism.* Retrieved from
http://articles.latimes.com/2011/oct/19/opinion/la-oe-
almarayati-fbi-20111019

[174] ibid.

[175] Reilly, Ryan. (2011, October 19). *DOJ: Holder 'Firmly
Committed' To Eliminating Anti-Muslim Training.* Retrieved
from http://talkingpointsmemo.com/muckraker/doj-official-
holder-firmly-committed-to-eliminating-anti-muslim-training

176 Islamic Terror on American Soil.
https://www.thereligionofpeace.com/attacks/american-attacks.aspx

177 Hate crime data collection guidelines, p. 24,
http://www.fbi.gov/about-us/cjis/ucr/hate-crime/hcguidelinesdc99.pdf accessed February 28, 2011.

178 18 U.S.C. § 2331 defines "international terrorism" and "domestic terrorism" for purposes of Chapter 113B of the U.S. Code, entitled "Terrorism." Retrieved from https://www.fbi.gov/investigate/terrorism

179 Volokh,Eugene. (June 26). *Chief Idaho federal prosecutor warns: "The spread of false information or inflammatory or threatening statements ... may violate federal law. Retrieved from* https://www.washingtonpost.com/news/volokh-conspiracy/wp/2016/06/26/chief-idaho-federal-prosecutor-warns-the-spread-of-false-information-or-inflammatory-or-threatening-statements-may-violate-federal-law/?utm_term=.21b2cc51e44e

180 Curtis, Michael. (2012, February 23). *Is Sharia Law Compatible with Democracy?* p.2 Retrieved from https://www.gatestoneinstitute.org/2869/sharia-law-democracy

181 ibid. p.1

182 ibid. p.1

183 ibid. p.3

[184] Hohmann, Leo. (2012, September 8). *Obama's '1st Muslim judge' has ties to Saudi regime.* Retrieved from http://www.wnd.com/2016/09/obamas-1st-muslim-judge-has-ties-to-saudi-regime/#3862M4b5B3z7uAlZ.99

[185] Hohmann, Leo. (2016, September 8). *Obama's '1st Muslim judge' has ties to Saudi regime.* Retrieved from http://mobile.wnd.com/2016/09/obamas-1st-muslim-judge-has-ties-to-saudi-regime/

[186] Poole, Patrick, Schmitz, Joseph & Team B II. *Sharia: The Threat to America, And Exercise in Competitive Analysis.* Center for Security Policy Press. October 2010 p. 2

[187] ibid. p.2

[188]https://www.thereligionofpeace.com/pages/Qur'an/taqiyya.aspx

[189] https://en.wikipedia.org/wiki/Linda_Sarsour

[190] Poole, Patrick, Schmitz, Joseph & Team B II. (2010, October) *Sharia: The Threat to America: An Exercise in Competitive Analysis. p. 7.* Retrieved from https://www.centerforsecuritypolicy.org/upload/wysiwyg/article%20pdfs/Shariah%20-%20The%20Threat%20to%20America%20(Team%20B%20Report)%20Web%2009292010.pdf

[191] Mohamad, Akram. (1991, May 22). *An Explanatory Memorandum: On the General Strategic Goal for the Group.* Government Exhibit 003-0085/3:04-CR-240-G U.S. v. HLF, et al.United States District Court, Northern District of Texas.

http://www.centerforsecuritypolicy.org/2013/05/25/an-explanatory-memorandum-from-the-archives-of-the-muslim-brotherhood-in-america/

[192] ibid. p. 74

[193] Quote of Taqi ad-Din Ahmed ibn Tamiyya, 13th-century Islamic jurist. (1263-1328). ibid. p. 75

[194] ibid. p.75

[195] Ibid. pp. 274-278 and appendix Explanatory Memorandum

[196] Hamas Charter Retrieved from http://www.terrorism-info.org.il/data/pdf/PDF_06_032_2.pdf

[197] Boykin, William, Soyster, Harry, Cooper Henry & 17 more. (2010, September 22). *Sharia: The Threat to America: An Exercise in Competitive Analysis (Report of Team B II)*. Center for Security Policy Press. p. 21. Print.

[198] The List

[199] Center for Security Policy. (n.d.). *Mapping the Muslim Brotherhood in America, a short course, part 16*. Retrieved from http://shariahthethreat.org/a-short-course-1-what-is-shariah/a-short-course-16-mapping-the-muslim-brotherhood-in-america/

[200] https://en.wikipedia.org/wiki/Mahmoud_Abbas

[201] http://www.jpost.com/Middle-East/Abbas-I-do-not-want-to-run-again-for-Palestinian-Authority-president-451689

202 http://www.aljazeera.com/news/2017/10/hamas-hands-gaza-border-crossings-pa-171031190038739.html

203 http://nypost.com/2017/04/30/mahmoud-abbas-harbors-terrorists-and-still-gets-a-white-house-welcome/

204 http://elderofziyon.blogspot.com/2015/07/dictator-abbas-grooming-saeb-erekat-to.html

205 Pavlich, Katie. (2016, September 9). *Funding Terrorism: US reportedly gave 33 billion to Iran, in cash and gold.* http://townhall.com/tipsheet/katiepavlich/2016/09/09/holy-crap-we-gave-30-billion-to-iranin-cash-n2216061

206 BBC News. (2003, June 9). *Who are Islamic Jihad?* Retrieved from http://news.bbc.co.uk/1/hi/world/middle_east/1658443.stm

207 Australian National Security. (2014, July 11). *Palestinian Islamic Jihad.* Retrieved from https://www.nationalsecurity.gov.au/Listedterroristorganisations/Pages/PalestinianIslamicJihad.aspx

208 Ben Gedalyahu, Tzvi. (2011, November 7). *Iran Backs Islamic Jihad's 8,000-Man Army in Gaza.* Retrieved from http://www.israelnationalnews.com/News/News.aspx/149498#.TrhgmnF4Vow

209 Bedeiin, David. (2005, August 10). *Do US Pressures Determine Israeli Policy?* Retrieved from http://israelbehindthenews.com/do-us-pressures-determine-israeli-policy/4615/

210 http://vision2030.gov.sa/en/node/149

[211] An IPO is an *initial public offering*, the very first sale of stock issued by a company to the public. To read more: https://www.investopedia.com/university/ipo/ipo.asp

[212] Ezekiel 38:13

[213] Hallinan, Conn. (2016, February1). *Adding Up The Cost of Hillary Clinton's Wars*. Retrieved from http://fpif.org/adding-costs-hillary-clintons-wars/

[214] Schweizer, Peter. (2016, May 1). *One Year of Silence On Hillary Clinton Wars*. Retrieved from http://www.breitbart.com/hillary-clinton/2016/05/01/one-year-silence-hillary-clinton-uranium-deal/

[215] Wehner, Peter. (2015, April). *Hillary Clinton's Bribery Scandal*. Retrieved from http://www.realclearpolitics.com/2015/04/26/hillary_clinton039s_bribery_scandal_355733.html

[216] Becker, Jo, McIntire, Mike. (2015, April 23). *Cash Flowed To the Clinton Foundation Amid Russian Uranium Deal*. Retrieved from http://www.nytimes.com/2015/04/24/us/cash-flowed-to-clinton-foundation-as-russians-pressed-for-control-of-uranium-company.html?_r=0

[217] Mandavia, Megha. (2016, October 21). *Rosatom opens regional centre in Mumbai*. Retrieved from www.nytimes.com/by/mike-mcintirehttp://economictimes.indiatimes.com/industry/energy/power/rosatom-opens-regional-centre-in-mumbai/articleshow/54977000.cms

[218] Mandavia, Megha. (2016, October 21). *Rosatom opens regional centre in Mumbai*. Retrieved fromhttp://economictimes.indiatimes.com/industry/energy/power/rosatom-opens-regional-centre-in-mumbai/articleshow/54977000.cms

[219] Breitbart News. (2016, August 23). AP: Many Donors to Clinton Foundation Met with Hillary at State. Retrieved from http://www.breitbart.com/2016-presidential-race/2016/08/23/ap-many-donors-clinton-foundation-met-hillary-state/

[220] http://www.publicationcoach.com/potemkin/

[221] https://www.nytimes.com/2017/01/23/us/politics/tpp-trump-trade-nafta.html

[222] Zaidi, Deena.(2016, July 8). *The Trans-Pacific Partnership: A Deal That Sanders, Clinton, and Trump All Oppose*. Retrieved fromhttp://www.truth-out.org/news/item/36752-the-trans-pacific-partnership-a-deal-that-sanders-clinton-and-trump-all-oppose

[223] Zaidi, Deena.(2016, July 8). *The Trans-Pacific Partnership: A Deal That Sanders, Clinton, and Trump All Oppose*. Retrieved from http://www.truth-out.org/news/item/36752-the-trans-pacific-partnership-a-deal-that-sanders-clinton-and-trump-all-oppose

[224] Zaidi, Deena.(2016, July 8). *The Trans-Pacific Partnership: A Deal That Sanders, Clinton, and Trump All Oppose*. Retrieved from http://www.truth-

out.org/news/item/36752-the-trans-pacific-partnership-a-deal-that-sanders-clinton-and-trump-all-oppose

[225] http://www.thehindu.com/news/international/south-china-sea-and-the-nine-dash-line-what-you-need-to-know/article14485046.ece1

[226]Lake, Eli. (2016, September 7). *Obama's Pivot To Asia Fails to Deter China*. Retrieved from https://www.bloomberg.com/view/articles/2016-09-07/obama-s-pivot-to-asia-fails-to-deter-china

[227] http://www.nydailynews.com/news/world/president-trump-granted-rare-dinner-china-forbidden-city-article-1.3618735

[228] Lake, Eli. (2016, September 7). *Obama's Pivot To Asia Fails to Deter China*. Retrieved from https://www.bloomberg.com/view/articles/2016-09-07/obama-s-pivot-to-asia-fails-to-deter-china

[229] https://www.bloomberg.com/view/articles/2016-09-07/obama-s-pivot-to-asia-fails-to-deter-china

[230] Plitsas, Alex. (2016, October 26). *Fact Check: Pence Was Right About Hillary Clinton's Failure In Iraq*. Retrieved from http://ijr.com/opinion/2016/10/260666-fact-check-pence-right-clintons-failure-renegotiate-iraq-forces-agreement/

[231] Chambers, Francesca. (2014, November 28). *America ditches decade-long plan to train a full-scale Iraqi army in favor of creating a small force actually able to fight ISIS – instead of running away from the militants.*

http://www.dailymail.co.uk/news/article-2853345/U-S-train-elite-force-Iraqis-fight-ISIS-instead-rebuilding-entire-army-again.html

[232] https://www.rt.com/op-edge/363539-civil-war-gaddafi-libya/

[233] Putz, Catherine, Tiezzi, Shannon. (2016, April 14). *Did Hillary Clinton's Pivot To Asia Work?*http://fivethirtyeight.com/features/did-hillary-clintons-pivot-to-asia-work/

[233] ibid.

Write me at hadas@hadassahjacobs.com

Check out my website and courses

www.hadassahjacobs.com

Follow me on . . .

Twitter:

https://twitter.com/hadasonpolitics

Linkedin:

https://www.linkedin.com/in/hadasjacobs/

Please write a review on Amazon!

Email me to receive your free gifts as a

Thank You for reading my book!

"Your past becomes your stepping stone for the future. The most important thing for you to do is, step."